Combatting Corruption at the Grassroots Level in Nigeria

Funso E. Oluyitan

Combatting Corruption at the Grassroots Level in Nigeria

Funso E. Oluyitan
Efon-Alaaye, Ekiti State
Nigeria

ISBN 978-3-319-44855-8   ISBN 978-3-319-44856-5 (eBook)
DOI 10.1007/978-3-319-44856-5

Library of Congress Control Number: 2016950014

© The Editor(s) (if applicable) and The Author(s) 2017
This work is subject to copyright. All rights are solely and exclusively licensed by the Publisher, whether the whole or part of the material is concerned, specifically the rights of translation, reprinting, reuse of illustrations, recitation, broadcasting, reproduction on microfilms or in any other physical way, and transmission or information storage and retrieval, electronic adaptation, computer software, or by similar or dissimilar methodology now known or hereafter developed.
The use of general descriptive names, registered names, trademarks, service marks, etc. in this publication does not imply, even in the absence of a specific statement, that such names are exempt from the relevant protective laws and regulations and therefore free for general use.
The publisher, the authors and the editors are safe to assume that the advice and information in this book are believed to be true and accurate at the date of publication. Neither the publisher nor the authors or the editors give a warranty, express or implied, with respect to the material contained herein or for any errors or omissions that may have been made.

Cover illustration: Cover pattern © Melisa Hasan

Printed on acid-free paper

This Palgrave Macmillan imprint is published by Springer Nature
The registered company is Springer International Publishing AG
The registered company address is: Gewerbestrasse 11, 6330 Cham, Switzerland

I dedicate this book to my family: My wife: Iyabo, BSc; my children: Dapo, BEd, Olumide, BSc, Olubunmi, MBA, Ayodele, MEd, Damilola, MD, and Olatunde, BSc. They are my precious gifts and my cheerleaders.

Foreword

The author of this book, Dr. Funso Oluyitan, is a former colleague at the Ahmadu Bello University, Zaria, Nigeria, and a family friend. We have known and interacted with one another for close to 4 decades. It is therefore a great honour, unique privilege, and distinct pleasure for me to write the preface to an important and timely book. It is important because corruption is perhaps the biggest obstacle to Nigeria realizing its true potential as a great, rich, just nation—an example to the rest of Africa, a source of pride to the black race, and a leading member of the international community.

The book is also timely because with the coming into power, first as a military Head of State and now as a democratically elected President, Muhammadu Buhari is leading the fight against corruption from the front. In so doing, he is enjoying tremendous goodwill at home and abroad. At the same time, however, "corruption is fighting back," as the saying goes in Nigeria. Nonetheless, Buhari must not fail because that would be our collective failure as Nigerians. In order to win the war against corruption in Nigeria, however, it is essential to understand the genesis and dynamics of this dangerous obstacle to socioeconomic development of the country. In this regard, corruption is not a new phenomenon. Indeed, as a scholar, Mathew Page of the US Council of Foreign Relations observed, "as far back as 1950 Abubakar Tafawa Balewa (who later became the first Prime Minister of Nigeria) decried the twin curses of bribery and corruption which pervaded every rank and department." From the relatively humble beginnings, however, corruption has grown in gigantic proportions throughout military and democratic dispensations in Nigeria.

Dr. Oluyitan's focus, as clearly demonstrated in this book, is on the duty of every citizen and individual responsibility as perhaps the best and most enduring strategy for defeating corruption. Through his own leadership by example and by sensitizing and encouraging citizens to take an "oath" against taking or given bribes and engaging in corruption, Dr. Oluyitan shows that practical grassroots efforts can work in addressing the scourge of corruption, which impedes the delivery of social services such as education and health, building of physical infrastructures, and overall development of Nigeria.

This book should be made compulsory reading for all aspirants to public offices in Nigeria at the local, state, and federal levels. It is also a useful handbook for all public officials, business leaders, and the citizens of Nigeria. Fighting corruption is a task for all, and, with the correct strategy, victory is possible.

Abuja, Nigeria   Professor Ibrahim A. Gambari

Acknowledgements

This book is the result of a dissertation I wrote for my second doctoral degree, a PhD in Leadership and Change, for Antioch University, Yellow Springs, Ohio, USA, specializing in the theory and practice of anti-corruption.

I am grateful to the following people: Chair, Dr. Philomena Essed, and the Committee of Dr. Lize Booysen, both of Antioch University, Professor Iyorwuese Hagher, Nigerian former minister and ambassador, and external reader, Dr. Karin Sporre of Umea University, Umea, Sweden, all of whom I thank for seeing my study on corruption in Nigeria through.

The 15 participant oath takers who took part in the various seminars I conducted in Nigeria and the United States between 1984 and 2013 remain anonymous, and I am grateful to them for creating the time to interact with me in collecting the data for the study.

At the end of the last hurdle, God sent Dr. Norman Dale of Canada to my path as my editor, indeed a competent and spontaneous editor.

Contents

1	**Introduction**	1
	The Universal Occurrence of Corruption	1
	About the Study	4
	Positionality: How the Oath Has Changed My Life	5
	The Genesis of Corruption in Nigeria: Colonialism to Independence	7
	Nationalism and Independence	9
	Nigeria's First Republic Through to the Present	11
	Development and Emergence of Modern Day Corruption	13
	Government and Non-Governmental Initiatives against Corruption	16
2	**Theoretical Overview on Corruption**	19
	Development, Modernization, and Corruption	20
	Manifestations of Corruption: Different Sectors, Different Agents	25
	How to Counter and Prevent Corruption (Government and Civil Society)	29
	Motivation: What It Means and Why Do People Get Involved in Civil Action?	32
	Maslow's Theory of Motivation	33
	Ethics and Moral Principles as Motivating Factors	38
	Development of Ethics/Moral Standards	40
	Oath and Religion	42
	Africa: Religion and Oath Taking	44

3 My Interviews with the Oath Takers — 53
The Story of My Life in This Study — 53
Why Narrative Inquiry? — 54
About the ANAC Seminars — 57
Data Gathering and Analysis — 59
The Selection and Interviewing of Participants for the Study — 63
Data Analysis — 66

4 Research Findings: Motives and Impacts of Oath Taking — 69
Motivating Factors — 70
Impacts of Taking the ANAC Oath — 76
Quantitative Summary of Motivating Factors for Oath Taking and Keeping — 84
Summary of Findings on Motivating Factors — 86

5 Discussion of Findings: Taking, Keeping and Violating the Oath — 89
What the Findings Reveal About Motivation — 90
Corruption Experienced or Witnessed and Consequent Resistance — 95
Commonalities from the Experience of the Participants — 98
Values of Revelation in Terms of Anti-Corruption Struggle — 101
How My Findings Relate to Motivation Theory and Thalhammer et al.'s Theory of Resistance — 101
Research Questions for the Future — 102

6 Policy and Practical Implications for Future Anti-Corruption Programs — 105
Role of Civil Organizations in Combating Corruption — 108
Final Thoughts — 111

References — 113

Index — 123

About the Author

Professor Funso Oluyitan assumed a role model for transparency in 1957 when he joined the then Nigerian League of Bribes Corner and embarked on a journey of transparent leadership. Oluyitan is a retired Professor of Communications and a Professor of Leadership and Change. A political science graduate of Bowie State University, Bowie, Maryland, he also attended Indiana University, Bloomington, Indiana, where he earned a Master's degree in public affairs/journalism and a Doctor of Education degree in instructional technology (radio and television production) in 1980. Thirty-six years later, in 2016, Professor Oluyitan earned a second doctoral degree, a PhD in Leadership and Change (combating corruption) from Antioch University, Yellow Spring, Ohio. He is the founder of the Association of Nigerians Against Corruption upon which the study in this book is based. He is also the author of *Africa Yesterday and Today,* published in 2007.

LIST OF FIGURES

Fig. 2.1   Maslow's hierarchy of needs theory   34
Fig. 5.1   Factors affecting and results of participants' keeping oath   91

LIST OF TABLES

Table 3.1	Profile of participants interviewed	64
Table 4.1	Categories of motivating factors and participant responses (used for Tables 4.2 and 4.3)	85
Table 4.2	Interview response data for motivating factors	86
Table 4.3	Interview response frequency for motivating factors	86

CHAPTER 1

Introduction

Abstract The chapter introduces the reader to the global occurrence of corruption and its genesis in Nigeria. It discusses corruption as defined by a number of scholars. It also introduces the reader to the reasons for conducting the study. The chapter narrates how the past has led to the spread and growth of corruption in Nigeria and describes initiatives to combat it.

Keywords Corruption · Immorality · Perversion · Dishonest · Misuse of power · Bribery · Favor · Moral depravity · No giver no receiver · Lord Lugard · Nationalism · Nigerian League of Bribes Corner · Nnamdi Azikiwe · Obafemi Awolowo · Ahmadu Bello · Aminu Kano · Joseph Tarka · Tafawa Balewa · Festus Okotiebo · Ladoke Akintola · Aguiyi-Ironsi · Yakubu Gowon · Mohammadu Buhari · Muritala Muhammad · Olusegun Obasanjo · Ibrahim Babangida · Sanni Abacha · Abdulsalam Abubakar · Shehu Shagari · Umaru Yar-Adua · Goodluck Jonathan · John Kerry · MAMSER · War against Indiscipline (WAI) · ICPC · Mustapha Akanbi · EFCC · Association of Nigerians against Corruption (ANAC)

THE UNIVERSAL OCCURRENCE OF CORRUPTION

This book is about corruption and efforts to combat it at the grassroots level in Nigeria. Corruption occurs at many levels from the highest political realms to the everyday person "on the street." In order for any nation to reduce corruption, it must be attacked simultaneously at all levels. Combating corruption at the grassroots level is one route to take, and perhaps literally the most fundamental.

The American Heritage College Dictionary (1993) defines "corrupt" as "1. Marked by immorality and perversion; depraved. 2. Venal or dishonest." Thereby, "corrupting" is "to ruin morally, pervert... to destroy or subvert the honesty or integrity of, as by offering bribes." These are human behaviors that exist in many forms and degrees across the world as actions of injustice. In its simplest form, corruption means to misuse power for private benefit or advantage. Besides money, the benefit can take the form of protection, special treatment, commendation, promotion, or other favors.

Otite (1986) opined that corruption "simply means the perversion of integrity or state of affairs through bribery, favor, or moral depravity" (p. 12). He explained that corruption involves the injection of additional but improper transactions aimed at changing the normal course of events and altering judgments and positions of trust. It consists of the doers', givers', and receivers' use of informal, extra-legal, or illegal acts to facilitate matters.

According to Transparency International (2006), corruption "affects all sectors of society from construction (France), education (Uganda), police (Malaysia), to parliament (Japan), judiciary (Brazil, Burkina Faso, Ecuador, Israel, and Nepal) and even the church (Greece)" (p. 119). Dreher et al. (2007) wrote in their study, "Corruption Around the World," "that corruption is the most significant contributor to low income and growth in many of the poor countries." Shleifer and Vishny (1993) had argued earlier that corruption is both pervasive and significant around the world and that "in some developing countries such as Zaire and Kenya it probably amounts to a large fraction of the Gross National Product" (p. 599). Gopinath (2008) agreed with the global concept when he wrote that corruption is a worldwide phenomenon, affecting developing and developed countries. The United Nations Office of Drugs and Crime (UNODC) made a similar observation:

> Corruption is a complex social, political, and economic phenomenon that affects all countries. Corruption undermines democratic institutions, slows economic development, and contributes to governmental instability. Corruption attacks the foundation of democratic institutions by distorting electoral processes, perverting the rule of law, and creating bureaucratic quagmires whose only reason for existing is the soliciting of bribes.

> Economic development is stunted because foreign direct investment is discouraged and small businesses within the country often find it impossible to overcome the "start-up costs" required because of corruption. (United Nations Office of Drugs and Crime, n.d.)

Corruption is an act by individuals or groups of individuals. The behavior is pronounced in Nigeria where corruption has become endemic and has a negative effect on every dimension of Nigerian life. Acutely embarrassing scandals have plagued the politics of Nigeria since the time of the colonial regime and even more so since independence in 1960.

> Nigeria is often perceived as the "giant of Africa" by most Africans, perhaps, because of its remarkable achievements in the continent in the past three decades. Today, the same country is looked upon by the rest of the world as a "crippled" giant, a veritable modern moral wasteland, a nation where corruption is extolled as a national culture, tradition; as a nation of business scams and fraudulent investment and contractual opportunities. (Ojukwu and Shopeju 2010, p. 12)

In spite of a series of laws and reforms directed at waging war against corruption in Nigeria, Transparency International (2014) still ranks Nigeria as one of the most corrupt countries in the world.

Given this debilitating and ubiquitous force, this book is about interventions *against* corruption in Nigeria. More particularly, the focus is on civil society interventions. Given the lack of progress in curtailing corruption from the side of the government, some anti-corruption organizations in Nigeria have recognized the need to appeal to the minds and moral agency of ordinary citizens in fighting corruption.

The involvement of civic organizations in combating corruption in Nigeria started even before the country gained independence in 1960. I became a member, in 1957, of one such organization, the Nigerian League of Bribes Corner through the encouragement of a class teacher, Mr. Olusegun Obasanjo (later Head of State and two-time president of Nigeria), during a discussion on corruption in a religious knowledge class. In order to be a member, an individual had to swear not to give or take a bribe and not to participate in any corrupt practices for the rest of his or/her life. I took the oath. This oath had a series of impacts on my life, one of which is that I later established the Association of Nigerians against Corruption (ANAC), a non-governmental organization (NGO). That was on 18 June 1984 while I was a senior lecturer at Ahmadu Bello University, Zaria. The group was founded as a complement to the War Against Indiscipline (WAI) program of the then-military government headed by Major General Muhammadu Buhari (who was elected president of Nigeria in 2015).

ANAC believes that if there is no giver of bribes and undue favors, there will be no receiver. Thus, the approach has been one of encouraging individuals to take a public oath not to give or receive bribes nor participate in any corrupt practices for the rest of their lives.

ANAC has been conducting seminars on corruption in several Nigerian cities and in the United States since 1984. Many Nigerians—my estimate would be close to 1000 Nigerians—have taken oaths similar to the one I first took in 1957. The present study is inspired by the impact the oath has had on my own life and is focused on selected others of Nigerian background who have taken a similar oath through ANAC seminars.

Studying what has transpired in the lives of oath takers before and after taking the oath is significant in understanding why they took the oath and if or how it has transformed their lives.

About the Study

The study from which this book is written examined why people take a voluntary public oath to shun corruption in all its ramifications. The answer to this question creates sub-questions that the study also tried to answer: What happened in their lives to make them come to that decision? How does taking the oath impact their lives? What motivates them once they have taken the oath? What role do family, religion, and peers play in the way they give meaning to the oath?

Answers to these questions came from individuals' life experiences. According to George et al. (2007), "Your life story provides the context for your experiences, and through it, you can find the inspiration to make an impact in the world" (p. 132). Frank (2010), in his book Letting *Stories Breathe*, further elaborated on several capacities that life stories can reveal or enable. They include character development, inherent morality, and truth telling, which undoubtedly devolves into more specific capacities revealed in storytelling.

The stories of participants are the sources of data for the study. It is recognizable that the life story interview (Atkinson 1998), being subjective, lends itself to interpretative data collection and analysis. The trustworthiness of the storyteller, the accuracy of the story, and the internal consistency of the stories were part of the bases for the formulation and collection of data.

The study took a unique approach to the problem of corruption. As compared to studies that have the economic approach of tallying up the stunning costs of corruption or that report depressingly on the breadth of the phenomenon—for example, from the United Nations in relation to the Convention against Corruption (UNODC, n.d.), this study provides understanding of a different and more personal kind. As the focus is on the act of taking an oath—which is not a common contemporary practice—and what that entails in the life of the oath taker, the study becomes an unusual story of personal moral behavior and what influences it. In sum, it combines looking at personal moral agency and its background, linked with the struggle over corruption. It clearly has the potential to bring new insights to the phenomenon of corruption.

Positionality: How the Oath Has Changed My Life

As founder and executive director of the Association of Nigerians against Corruption (ANAC), I am not a neutral party in the research. Emphasis will be on the progress made in a colossal ongoing battle, not on "objectively" critiquing the initiative. ANAC's goals include:

- Campaign against bribery and corruption with its entire ramifications in Nigeria;
- Instill in Nigerian youths in colleges, polytechnics, universities, and other tertiary institutions in Nigeria the virtues of a corruption-free society;
- Encourage Nigerian youths in higher institutions in Nigeria to make public declarations against bribery and corruption; and
- Organize workshops, conferences, seminars, symposia, and public lectures to sensitize and raise public awareness on bribery and corruption and the need to shun bribery and corruption and all related vices in Nigeria.

Since its establishment, ANAC has conducted eight of its seminars in Nigeria and among Nigerians in Dayton, Ohio, and New York City. The oath takers at these seminars make up the population in the study.

Generally, non-governmental organizations' (NGOs) ultimate goals are to change societal norms, improve understanding, influence agendas, influence policies, and solve problems where adequate actions are absent on the part of the government (Fisher 1998); however, most of the NGOs in Nigeria have done less in addressing official corruption cases, and many have also become vulnerable to corruption themselves (Otusanya 2011).

It is against the background of ANAC initiatives as an NGO working to combat corruption that my dissertation research, and ultimately the work on this book, has unfolded. Oath taking is a key concept of the theoretical frame of the research. What motivates people to take an oath against corruption and to live, sometimes with great difficulty and even at personal risk, according to that oath?

I took the oath that I will not give or take bribe and will not participate in any corrupt practices for the rest of my life in December 1957 at the age of 17. In the midst of many temptations, either as a customs officer, a journalist (both print and electronic), a special police officer in the US, or as a university lecturer in Nigeria and the US, I am proud to write that I have kept my oath.

After high school, I had opportunities to work at jobs with a lot of tempting under-the-table activities. My upbringing and my spirituality kicked in. I resigned from being a customs officer because of the temptation. I finally settled for the job of my dreams when I became a reporter for a national newspaper, *The Nigerian Morning Post*. Yet opportunities to be corrupt also existed at this job and still occur in many media jobs in Nigeria. I found myself leading some other journalists by rejecting the bribe, often tagged as "the brown envelope," often slyly offered after news conferences. After a short experience as a newspaper reporter, I joined the national radio station, the Nigerian Broadcasting Corporation, as a music librarian. This position put me in another situation of test and challenge to my upbringing and faith. It was my duty to decide which new music record releases would be aired and which would not, indeed a lucrative position to be corrupted. Music artists stormed the studio to promote frequent playing of their new releases. Promoters and record sellers curried my favor and were not approaching me empty-handed. They came with the classic brown envelopes and other gifts to influence my decision. I always passed the test of my upbringing, the test of my oath, the test of who I am. Duval and Wicklund (as cited in Gardner et al. 2005) stated that self-awareness represents an attentive state where the individual directs his or her conscious attention to some aspect of the self. They argued that by learning, by doing, who you are and what you value, you build understanding and a sense of self that provides a firm anchor for your decisions and actions.

At the completion of a master's degree in public affairs and journalism in the US, a rare opportunity opened up for me: I was employed as a special police officer by the Indianapolis Police Department as part of a victim assistance program launched by the then-mayor of Indianapolis, Richard Lugar. Here again I witnessed a lopsided approach to duty and unprofessional performances among some police officers. Temptations abounded for me. My upbringing and spirituality, sealed by my oath, always kicked in for me. On 22 November 1976, a year and a half after my appointment with the Indianapolis Police Department, I was selected as Officer of the Month.

The above are just snapshots of a long life with many challenges to my integrity. Like Bell (2002), through ethical ambition, I found it possible to avoid compromising myself in the face of every opportunity to get ahead by accepting illicit favors. Bell noted that trying to simultaneously balance dreams and needs is tough and requires an unending assessment of who you are and what you believe, value, and desire.

In writing this book, and retelling the stories of real and hard choices, I want to leave a legacy for the generations after me. I understand the meaningfulness of integrity and the impact of the oath on my life but want to know how the oath works for others. What can young people learn from this?

In order for the reader to appreciate the broader social significance of the title of this book, I now provide an overview of the historical context of corruption and anti-corruption interventions in Nigeria.

The Genesis of Corruption in Nigeria: Colonialism to Independence

Nigeria is composed of over 350 ethnic groups with distinct identities and histories dating back to prehistoric times. After the European discovery of the West Coast of Africa in the fifteenth century, the British established bases along the coasts of what later came to be called Nigeria. They engaged vigorously in the exploration and exploitation of the territory (Dzoho 2007). The abolition of the slave trade in the nineteenth century brought the British naval squadrons to the shores of Nigeria, Liberia, and Sierra Leone to police slave traders. European activities revolved around four major issues: exploration, Christianity, trade, and imperialism (Ajayi 1962; Falola 1999). At the same time that the British were gaining ground from the southern coastal area, the northern part of Nigeria was also coming increasingly under the influence and authority of Islam; this created the Sokoto caliphate in that part of the country. British interest in colonization manifested as it established a consulate in Lagos in 1861.

The British conquest of Nigeria occurred in two stages: the southern phase from 1850 to 1897 and the northern phase from the turn of the century to 1914. Diplomacy and force were the key tools, with local leaders responding with similar tactics or merely surrendering to defeat (Falola 1999). In 1900, Lord Frederick Lugard, a former captain in the West African Frontier Force, raised the Union Jack as High Commissioner for Northern Nigeria. In 1912, he was appointed the governor of the Colony and Protectorate of Southern Nigeria and of the Protectorate of Northern Nigeria. There were three autonomous territories, two in the south and one in the north. On 1 January 1914, Lord Lugard amalgamated the territories together into one country, Nigeria, under the rule of a British governor-general (Falola 1999). The Federal Government of Nigeria commemorated 100 years of this amalgamation in January 2014.

Lord Lugard pioneered indirect rule in Nigeria, thereby anchoring racial dualism in a politically enforced ethnic pluralism (Mamdani 1996). Lugard empowered the local chiefs (emirs) to continue ruling their subjects and exercise administrative rule while the Europeans dictated what they wanted to the local chiefs and got things done without facing the people they governed. According to Falola (1999), Lord Lugard had observed how indirect rule worked in practice in colonial India and the Sudan. Comparing the emirates in northern Nigeria with political institutions in the Sudan, he concluded that indirect rule would serve colonial interests well in Nigeria too. The policy of indirect rule was designed to secure the cooperation of indigenous rulers and their people (Falola 1999). Approaching the people through their local leaders meant that opposition to British rule would become minimal, allowing local leaders to exercise administrative power, while the British manipulated them surreptitiously. Thus, the emirs were to become collaborators with and servants of colonialism through generous rewards and favors. The stage for today's corruption issues was set.

Commenting on this concept of indirect rule, Mamdani (1996) described the colonial state as a double-sided affair in which one side of governing is through corrupt customary authorities and the other side a regime of extra-economic coercion and administratively driven justice.

The outcome of indirect rule was the increase in the power of chiefs far more than tradition allowed, thus promoting abuse of power and tyranny. People had no power to remove unpopular kings and chiefs who owed their allegiance to the foreign government that had appointed them. Supporting staffs of the native authorities came to be power wielders rather than public servants. "They demanded respect, collected bribes, and offered services as favors" (Falola 1999, p. 24).

One economic objective of British rule was to make Nigeria financially self-sufficient, ensuring that the colony was profitable for both the colonizer and indigenous leaders. Infrastructures for transportation (harbors, roads, railways) and communications (telegraphic, postal) were developed to connect production sites with harbors to facilitate raw material extraction and exportation. As the railways and roads improved the mobility of goods, people, and ideas, production of raw materials increased. The distribution of imported items was facilitated with rural markets connected to the urban centers and the port cities. New currencies promoted the growth of wage income and increased trade transaction. The roads and railways promoted inter-group interaction and aided massive population movements from the villages to the cities. According to Dike (1999), the economy of Nigeria was oriented toward production for the external market.

NATIONALISM AND INDEPENDENCE

Resistance to White rule in Nigeria began in the church where Blacks were not allowed to serve as pastors. According to Ayegboyin and Ishola (1997), Edward Blyden called on Africans to establish their own independent churches primarily in opposition to European control. An example was the African Church Denomination founded by J. K. Coker in 1901 because of inhuman treatment meted to African clergy by Anglican missionaries.

Nationalism could be said to have been accelerated by colonial rule as notable changes of the era—such as urbanization, Western education, and transportation—contributed to the growth of nationalist activities. Newspapers, magazines, and other information circulated to influence opinions. Falola (1999) noted that one of the early heroes on nationalist issues was John Payne Jackson, originally a Liberian, who lived in Lagos,

Nigeria, from 1890 to 1918 and was the publisher of *Lagos Weekly Record*. He supported demands for reforms and called for unity among Nigerians to fight the British. Nigerian students studying abroad formed associations with the objectives of fostering national consciousness, racial pride, and reforms, among others. One formidable student at the time was Nnamdi Azikiwe, first president of the Republic of Nigeria, from 1960 to 1966. He studied in the US (1923–1932) and returned to Nigeria to join the struggle for "a government of the people by the people for the people" as he described it in my 2008 television interview with him at Lincoln University, his alma mater (Oluyitan and Azikiwe 2013).

After returning home from Lincoln University, Pennsylvania, in 1932, Azikiwe became a prominent member of the Nigerian Youth Movement, which he joined in 1937. In the same year he established the *West African Pilot*, a paper whose editorials focused on the themes of colonial injustice, exploitation, and racism. Azikiwe contributed to the rise of militant nationalism and combative journalism. Drawing on his experience in the United States, he saw the struggles in Nigeria as between Blacks and Whites and called for a united front against the British (Azikiwe 1994).

The birth of political parties that led Nigeria to independence began in 1944 when the Nigerian National Council (NNC) was formed with Herbert Macaulay as president and Nnamdi Azikiwe as Secretary General. To allow the admittance of a Cameroonian in Lagos to the party, Southern Cameroon, which was then part of Nigeria, brought on a change in the name of the party to the National Association of Nigerians and the Cameroons (NCNC). Other political parties emerged with regional roots that eventually led to the emergence of regionally based political parties. In the west, the Action Group (AG) emerged, being led by Obafemi Awolowo under the auspices of a cultural Yoruba organization, *Egbe Omo Yoruba*.

In the north the Northern People's Congress (NPC), headed by Ahmadu Bello, used Islam to create a solid party for the north. The Northern Elements Progressive Union (NEPU) headed by Mallam Aminu Kano and the United Middle Belt Congress (UMBC) headed by Joseph Tarka also emerged in the north. Memberships in these parties relied largely on ethnic composition; thus, the foundation for political parties was recognized as the Hausa, Ibo, and Yoruba parties. Personally, as one who was a print and radio journalist in the first 9 years of Nigeria as a free nation, I can attest to the ethnic identification of the parties. Leaders of the political parties led several delegations to London to argue for

Nigeria's independence from Britain. On 1 October 1960, Nigeria attained independence and became a republic in 1963.

In his book *Nigeria in Quagmire*, Ejiofor (2010) wrote:

> At Independence on October 1, 1960, Nigerian political leaders found themselves caught in the mud. They were hardly well trained intellectually and politically to captain the ship of a twentieth century nation state. Expectedly it was impossible for them to advance the new independent nation beyond the frontiers of our colonial heritage—degeneracy and corruption. (p. 10)

NIGERIA'S FIRST REPUBLIC THROUGH TO THE PRESENT

Nigeria's constitution after independence in 1960 was fashioned after the British Parliamentary system. There were lower and upper parliamentary houses and the leader of government—the prime minister in the federal system, the premier in the states, were chosen from the party that won a majority of seats in the election to the parliament. Prior to the declaration of independence a national election in 1959 catapulted three parties into power. The NPC won 134 seats, the NCNC 89, the AG 73, and the remaining 16 independent candidates (Falola 1999, p. 102). The Governor-General, Sir James Robertson, invited Tafawa Balewa of the NPC to form a government. The NPC and the NCNC formed a coalition government, and the AG became the opposition party. The executive was represented by a governor-general: Dr. Nnamdi Azikiwe became the first Nigerian governor-general. Nigeria consisted of three states, the Northern Region, Eastern Region, and Western Region, which had recognizable characteristics as Hausa, Ibo, and Yoruba states, respectively. After Nigeria became a republic in 1963, the head-of-state changed from a governor-general to a president. A new state, the Mid-Western State, was created from the Western Region.

As someone who witnessed the political events of Nigeria from independence and was also a newspaper reporter in the First Republic, I could describe Nigerian politics as dominated by both character and physical assassination. The task of those in power was to destroy the opposition. Solidarity and loyalty to those in power became the order of the day. Similar to modern events in South Africa reported by Ramphele (2012), solidarity and loyalty are major costs in the quality of democracy.

Apparently, in South Africa, as in Nigeria, loyalty to the party in power is awarded by undeserved contracts and disregard of unethical practices at various levels of the government, a practice that Ramphele described:

> Acquiescing to corrupt practices to advance one's business is both immoral and unethical. It is immoral in that it undermines the long term good for business and society in general. It is unethical because the corruptor knows that it is wrong to perpetuate corruption by rewarding those involved. Corruption is a cancer that threatens the sustainability of business and societies. (p. 75)

Such loyalty to those in power provides fertile ground for corruption in Nigeria. Falola (1999) confirmed that Nigerian politics was little concerned with good government or the reconciliation of competing demands. Rather, it was devoted primarily to primitive accumulation and extraction of resources to satisfy the demands of politicians.

Elsewhere, I have noted that, not long after independence, tribal differences became a compelling factor in Nigerian politics (Oluyitan 2007). Political crises that began in the Western Region led to a treason trial that landed the opposition leader, Chief Obafemi Awolowo, a 10-year jail term along with some of his Action Group lieutenants. Other issues, such as the census and statements of divine domination by one tribe over the other, led to controversy, which created chaos and unrest in the Western Region. The unrest was taking place when the wave of military interventions in the government was blowing through many post-colonial African countries. It was no surprise, therefore, that on 15 January 1966 a section of the Nigerian army staged a coup that killed Prime Minister Tafawa Balewa; Finance Minister, Festus Okotiebo; Premier of the Northern Region, Sir Ahmadu Bello; and his Western Region counterpart, Chief Samuel Ladoke Akintola. It was the beginning of a chain of military coups that was to besiege Nigeria—and lead to a 3-year civil war (Oluyitan 2007).

The mantle of Nigerian leadership has passed from General Aguiyi-Ironsi to General Yakubu Gowon to Generals Muhammadu Buhari, Muritala Muhammed, Olusegun Obasanjo, Ibrahim Babangida, Sanni Abacha, and Abdulsalam Abubakar between 1966 and 1998. In between, Alhaji Shehu Shagari served one full 4-year term as an elected president before being overthrown in the early part of his second term. General Olusegun Obasanjo came back as an elected civilian president after winning in a 1999 election. Obasanjo was re-elected for a second term in April 2003.

On 29 May 2007, he handed power over to a newly elected president, Umaru Yar'Adua. President Yar'Adua died in office on 5 May 2010, and his vice president Goodluck Jonathan was sworn in to complete the term. President Jonathan was elected in 2011 and sought re-election in March 2015, but Nigerians chose his opponent, a former military head of state, retired Major General Muhammadu Buhari, as president for a four-year term.

DEVELOPMENT AND EMERGENCE OF MODERN DAY CORRUPTION

The genesis of corruption in Nigeria dates back to the era of colonialism as described above. The indirect rule that created the establishment of Local Authorities, appointment of Warrant Chiefs, and Interpreters in the 1900s created a new cohort of Nigerians who exploited their fellow citizens under the protection of their British superiors. Colonialism tore apart a culture that was democratic, wherein group decision-making and sharing resources among individuals and villagers prevailed; foreign rule created new attitudes toward material wealth (Ishichei 1976). Korieh and Njoku (2007) noted that the advent of the structures of European colonialism invented an uneven socio-political landscape, placing public officers over their communities and thus reducing the powers of the people to exercise a meaningful pressure on their public figures or calling them to order. This created a breeding ground for the endemic socio-political corruption, which has become a monster in African societies. "When the British granted Nigeria independence in 1960, the emergent leadership was bedeviled with ineffectiveness, tribalism, sectionalism and corruption" (Dzoho 2007, p. 2).

As already stated, since becoming an independent country, Nigeria has been governed by 13 leaders, 8 of whom were military leaders. Since independence, Nigeria has been a quagmire due to corruption and bad leadership by most of those who were elected to rule—and notably by those who forced their ways to power through the barrels of guns (Ejiofor 2010). The 2010 Global Monitoring Report (GMR) of the United Nations Education, Scientific, and Cultural Organization (UNESCO) confirmed the nature and impacts of corruption in Nigeria, stating that the quality of life of most Nigerians has been progressively on the decline (United Nations Education, Scientific and Cultural Organization 2010). The UNESCO report stipulated that while the large majority of Nigerians continue to wallow in abject poverty, a privileged few live in opulence. "Poverty has, indeed become the face of Nigeria and poses a serious threat to the development of the country" (p. 1). A former Nigerian ambassador and author, Hagher (2011), wrote:

> Nigeria, the most populous African country with over 150 million people, is cited by foreign diplomats and journalists as a classic case of a country in the twilight zone. A basket case teetering towards collapse, on the margin of being declared a failed state. (p. 6)

It is common to find headlines like the following regularly in Nigerian newspapers:

- Nigerian politician accused of embezzling $100M
- Ten former governors stole $250 billion in three years
- Nigeria lost N36tr (36 Trillion Nigerian Naira) to corruption in 40 years

Where is the stolen wealth coming from? "The gifts of nature bestowed on this country in west coast of Africa and the existence of now many white elephant institutions make this catalogue of woes an incomprehensible paradox," wrote Ejiofor (2010, p. 41). He continued: "Nigeria is blessed with crude oil, gold, columbine, tin, coal, diamond. The land surface is massive and arable. There are numerous life sustaining rivers and waters with the luxury of the Atlantic Ocean at its southern border" (p. 41).

Corruption, lack of transparency, lack of accountability, and lack of good governing are the demise of many African countries, of which Nigeria is but one. Dzoho (2007) stated that the successive military regimes of Nigeria had ensured complete corruption of the body politic and all social institutions of the country "whether judiciary, police, election regulation, banks, ministries in government, churches, mosques, traditional ruler-ships, marriage, education, hospitals, etc." (p. 10). He wrote:

> Every facet of society has been thoroughly corrupted, as such, the highest bidder gets his way, and morality is the worse for it. Self-respect, ideologies, standards, norms, principles, etc. are all easily compromised daily, as nearly everyone in the Nigerian society is out to grab his share of the national cake. (p. 10)

He concluded that this situation had created confusion and despair in the Nigerian society, requiring urgent sanitization. Hagher (2011) further explained:

> Within the first few years of Nigeria's independence it became clear that the nation was richly endowed with a curse; the blood of the earth called oil. This curse thwarted development, exacerbated greed, and subverted democracy and has been the chief cause of corruption in Nigeria. (p. 76)

Smith (2006), in an introduction to his book, *A Culture of Corruption*, wrote that the government-controlled oil industry was riddled with graft and that beginning in the 1980s Nigeria was also believed to be a transit hub in the international narcotics trade, with widespread allegations of official collusion. "The country's image as a bastion of bribery, venality, and deceit has remained constant over the years" (p. 1). He wrote that the global expansion of the Internet has delivered evidence of Nigerian fraud to the e-mail inboxes of millions of people around the world.

A report submitted to the United States Congress by Secretary of State John Kerry put corruption in Nigeria in its proper perspective. *Country Reports on Human Rights Practices for 2012* (US Department of State, Bureau of Democracy, Human Rights & Labor 2012) stated that massive, widespread, and pervasive corruption affected all levels of government and even the security forces in Nigeria. Noting that though Nigerian law provides criminal penalties for official corruption, the report stated, "Government did not implement the law effectively, and officials frequently engaged in corrupt practices with impunity" (p. 39). Several cases of financial scandals were chronicled in the report, which estimated government money lost to endemic corruption and entrenched inefficiency to $6.8 billion. The report cited several cases of corruption involving members of national assembly, state governors, and cabinet ministers, among others.

Depressing assessments of Nigeria's situation as arising from corruption have also come from within. The political scientist Omololu Fagbadebo of Obafemi Awolowo University in Ile-Ife has reviewed the origins and contemporary effects of corruption, concluding on the vulnerability of the nation as a result:

> A failed, corrupt and inept leadership coupled with inclement domestic socio-political environment have plunged development performance in

Nigeria into the abyss. Development is no longer what the people desire, but what the creditor nations and international financial institutions dictate. The domestic policy-making process is now imported from abroad... (Fagbadebo 2007, p. 35)

The long and hard-fought dreams of real independence have been gravely jeopardized by endemic, seemingly irresolvable corruption.

GOVERNMENT AND NON-GOVERNMENTAL INITIATIVES AGAINST CORRUPTION

The war against corruption is one of the main and inevitable rationales given in the long string of "emergency" take-overs through military coups in Nigeria. The *State Security (Detention of Persons) Decree* in 1984 and the *Recovery of Public Property Special Military Tribunals Decree* were promulgated ostensibly to prohibit fraudulent enrichment by public servants (Kofele-Kale 2006); however, anti-corruption crusades by the military government did not fight corruption within its own army and so did not achieve much that positively affected the average citizens. Different administrations established different agencies to curb corruption, including the Mass Mobilization for Social Justice and Economic Recovery (MAMSER), the National Open Apprenticeship (NOA), the National Orientation Agency, and the War against Indiscipline (WAI). As a witness to most of the military governments, I was repeatedly appalled by the reckless and authoritarian lifestyle of those in uniform that became the expected order of the day.

After the return to elected government in 1999, President Obasanjo established two commissions to wage war against corruption. The resolve to fight and win the war against corruption led to the promulgation of the *Corrupt Practices and Other Related Offences Act* (2000), which established the Independent Corrupt Practices and Other Related Offences Commission (ICPC). The commission, first headed by Justice Mustapha Akanbi, was mandated to prohibit and prescribe punishments for corrupt practices and other related offences. As the preponderance of economic and financial crimes such as advance fee fraud and money laundering showed severe negative consequences on Nigeria, including decreased foreign direct investment, a second anti-corruption commission was established. The Economic and Financial Crimes Commission (EFCC) was established in 2004. The act mandated the EFCC to combat financial and economic crimes. The commission is empowered to prevent, investigate, prosecute, and penalize economic and financial wrongdoing and is charged with the responsibility of enforcing the provisions of other laws and regulations relating to economic and financial crimes, including: the *Money Laundering Act* (1995), the *Money Laundering Prohibition Act* (2004), the *Advanced Fee Fraud and Other Fraud Related Offences Act* (1995), the *Failed Banks Recovery of Debts and Financial Malpractices in Banks Act* (1994), the *Banks and other Financial Institutions Act* (1991), and the *Miscellaneous Offences Act* (1992). Though some well-known politicians and government officials have been prosecuted and jailed, corruption is still pervasive in the country.

As stated in a US Department of State, Bureau of Democracy, Human Rights & Labor (2012) assessment, Nigerian law provides criminal penalties for official corruption, but the government does not implement the law effectively; officials, the report concludes, have frequently engaged in corrupt practices with impunity. Nigerian Senator Smart Adeyemi (2013) has called for a third anti-graft agency to monitor the financial activities of all political office holders in the country. He stressed the need for more anti-graft agencies to combat the widespread of corruption in every sector of the Nigerian society. Such an independent body should monitor and look into the affairs of political office holders by monitoring their banking activities and standard of living. In a true democracy, this measure would be intrusive on the freedom of individual citizens.

The EFCC claimed that under its previous chairman, Nuhu Ribadu, the agency had addressed financial corruption by prosecuting and convicting a number of high-profile corrupt individuals, ranging from Nigeria's former chief law enforcement officer to several bank chief executives (see Fabiyi and Adetayo 2012). By 2005, the EFCC had arrested government officials including a former state governor. In September 2006, the EFCC had 31 of Nigeria's 36 state governors under investigation for corruption. In April 2008, the EFCC began investigating influential politicians and ministers for money stolen under their watch.

The fight against corruption is not for the government alone. Leaders arise from and reflect their origins among the everyday people of Nigeria. It is a task that must be confronted by the people of the whole nation. There are several Non-Government Organizations against corruption in Nigeria. One such is the Association of Nigerians against Corruption (ANAC). The NGOs against corruption in Nigeria are under the umbrella of the Zero Corruption Coalition (ZCC), which constitutes a network of 50 organizations campaigning against corruption in Nigeria. The ZCC also does advocacy work with legislators and government anti-corruption agencies on the need to domesticate and implement both the United Nations and the African Union Convention on Corruption.

All attempts to curb corruption in Nigeria have focused on government and non-government organization initiatives against corruption. None of these initiatives, except ANAC, focus on attacking the problem from the grassroots level by advocating for campaigns against corruption and encouraging commitment at the individual level. My research therefore uses the individual approach, tapping on the motivation, ethics, morality, and religion of each individual to be committed to a corruption-free life.

CHAPTER 2

Theoretical Overview on Corruption

Abstract This chapter is a literature review on corruption. It includes an overview of relevant research on corruption and key concepts and theories guiding the study, including Maslow's famous "Hierarchy of Needs" and Thalhammer et al.'s framework of Courageous Resistance. The chapter further reviews literature relating corruption to morality and ethics, motivation, religion, oath taking, and family upbringing. It examines a range of initiatives from both government and civil society, designed to prevent and counter corruption.

Keywords International Country Risk Guide (ICGR) · World Development Report (WDR) · Global Competitiveness Survey (GCS) · Country Risk Review (CRR) · Corruption Perception Index (CPI) · Giorgio Blundo · Jean-Pierre Oliver de Sardan · United Nations Convention against Corruption · Habibie · Abdurrahman Wahid · Corruption Practice Investigation Bureau (CPIB) · Independent Commission against Corruption (ICAC) · Maslow's Theory of Motivation · Boko Haram · Moral standards · Ethical behavior · Oath taking · Mbiti · Ubuntu

To situate the work presented in this book, we must first overview related research on corruption and key concepts, and the theories guiding the study of this book are also discussed. Such terms and concepts include corruption, morality and ethics, motivation, religion, oath taking, and family upbringing.

Development, Modernization, and Corruption

Though corruption is widespread, it is not the same everywhere. Sizeable literature has emerged explaining corruption in different countries around the world. Some corruption indices were published in the late 1970s and 1980s (Habib and Zurawicki 2001). This spawned empirical and quantitative research on a variety of corruption-related issues. Because of its clandestine nature, collecting data on corruption often relies on individual perceptions of country experts or business people with extensive experience in the countries in question. Owing to the difficulty of empirically observing corruption, many if not most researchers have used experimental methods to show the workings of corruption (see Banuri and Eckel 2012 for a review of such studies).

Corruption data have been generated by several organizations including the following listed by Lederman et al. (2005):

1. The International Country Risk Guide (ICRG) measures corruption as the likelihood that government officials (both high- and low-ranking) would demand and/or accept bribes in exchange for special licenses, policy protection, biased judicial sentences, avoidance of taxes and regulations, or simply to expedite government procedures. The index is based on the analysis of a worldwide network of experts and treats corruption mainly as a threat to foreign investment.
2. The World Development Report (WDR) uses a similar definition and treats corruption as an obstacle to business in general.
3. The index calculated by GALLUP International uses a survey of citizens to measure the frequency of cases of corruption among public officials.
4. The Global Competitiveness Survey (GCS) indices measure the frequency of irregular payment connected with imports, exports, business licenses, police protection, loan applications, and so on. GCS is a business executive's survey.
5. The Country Risk Review (CRR-DRI) index is part of Standard & Poor's credit rating system for emerging markets. It uses analysts'

opinions to measure the prevalence of corruption among public officials and the effectiveness of anti-corruption initiatives. (pp. 8–9)

Habib and Zurawicki (2001) added that the Corruption Perception Index (CPI) is produced by Transparency International, a non-governmental organization involved in the fight against corruption worldwide.

Buchner et al. (2008) conducted a laboratory experiment to study the granting of procurement contracts by a bureaucrat who is interested in providing a low price in return for a bribe from the provider. Their experiment set up a situation where the bidders compete by choosing prices and bribes simultaneously. The result was a correlation between price and bribe decisions and a discouraging and meaningful conclusion:

> When confronted with a corrupt bureaucracy, even framing bribes as socially detrimental does not prevent engaging in active bribery, at least when there is no threat of (legal) punishment... being aware that corruption is detrimental for society does not help much. (Buchner et al. 2008, p. 116)

The fact that this result arose in an artificial role-playing context underlines the challenges of individual tendencies that my work and research are intended to counteract.

Back in the real world, a World Bank study (Iarossi and Clarke 2011) conducted in 26 states of Nigeria indicated that about 80 % of businesses in Nigeria paid bribes to government officials. Gyimah-Brempong (2002), in a study within several African nations, found that corruption decreases economic growth directly and indirectly through decreased investment in physical capital. The author compared the interpretation of corruption in Africa to particular practices in developed countries. In his extensive literature review on corruption, he questioned the bias of rich countries in perceptions of what constitutes a bribe when he asked:

> When does a gift to a public official become a bribe? To what extent is money given to an African public official to influence policy (which is considered bribery) different from a contribution to a congressional campaign by lobbyists in the United States? (p. 190)

Notwithstanding such important caveats, Gyimah-Brempong concluded that corruption has a large negative and statistically significant impact on the growth rate of income in African countries.

Ksenia (2008), focusing on developing countries, described three types of corruption:

1. Bureaucratic corruption when officials take bribes before performing services;
2. Political corruption when elected politicians use their position of power to influence decisions after taking bribes;
3. Grand corruption where head of states, ministers, and top officials take bribes and misuse their power for a gain.

Ksenia attributed symptoms of corruption such as poorly designed economic policies, low levels of education, underdeveloped civil society, and weak accountability of public institutions as the causes of the three types of corruption. She also discussed money laundering as corruption that drains the economy of a country and cited the president of the Financial Action Task Force, Gil Galvao, who had stated that money laundering causes "inexplicable changes." These include changes in money demand, increased prudential risks for the safety of the banking sector, negative effects on financial transaction, increased volatility of international capital flows exchange rate, and reduced rate of foreign direct investment. Political/public office holders are considered to be among the most corrupt leaders, and their names have been prominent in various articles in developing countries and the Western media on corruption and illicit money flows (see Otusanya 2011). Such crimes are frequently reported in Nigeria. One could pick a Nigerian newspaper up any day and always find something on corruption.

Lambsdorff's (1998) study, *An Empirical Investigation of Bribery in International Trade*, argued that international regulation of bribery of foreign officials has an effect on exporting countries that abide by the rules. He reported that, in October 1995, Commerce Secretary Ron Brown presented a CIA report to the US Congress, claiming that between 1994 and 1995 the US lost $36 billion of business deals because of bribery and corruption by its competitors. The literature reviewed by Lambsdorff showed ways in which bribery is conducted. These included dubious payments that cannot be documented and exporters offering expensive foreign trips or donating scholarships to family members of foreign officials. Bribery could also be delegated to local agents who claim ignorance when illicit benefits are uncovered. Another scheme works by having a local agent act as an intervening purchaser, bribing for the acquisition of a contract and then selling the contract to the foreign exporter.

Coker et al. (2012) discussed the investigation of the Halliburton case, which involved the US-based multinational funneling $180 million to Nigerian officials to get a major contract in development of a liquefied natural gas plant in Bonny Island in the Niger Delta. Jeffery Tesler, a British lawyer, who had served as the consortium's agent in Nigeria and the central figure in the alleged bribery scandal, agreed in his deposition to the investigating judge that he made payments to Nigerian officials that awarded the original contract to the consortium. His questionable words of regret speak volumes of the assumptions that outsiders feel justified to make about corruption in Nigeria:

> There is no day when I do not regret my weakness of character... I allowed myself to accept standards of behavior in a business culture which can never be justified. I accepted the system of corruption that existed in Nigeria. (quoted in Fitzgibbin 2015, para.1)

Lambsdorff (2003) looked at how corruption affects persistent capital flow using data from many countries, developed and not. Using data from the International Country Risk Guide (ICRG) and the data by Gastil (1986) on political rights and civil liberties, he tested all the variables for their potential to explain the chosen corruption index. The study broke down corruption into sub-components and determined which of the governance indicators are crucial to attracting capital inflows. The components are government stability, law and order, bureaucratic quality, and civil liberties. Government stability is insignificant as a result, meaning that it is not a crucial criterion for foreign investors. The case of Nigeria where corruption is highly rated is used as an example. Due to tight military control the leadership managed to be in power for such a long period that it was rated as stable by the International Country Risk Guide (ICRG). Lambsdorff (2003) called it "perfect kleptocracy" (p. 235), meaning a state predominantly run by corruption and thievery. Kleptocrats can secure and expand power but not commit to effective policies unless these "line their pockets." Investors therefore will be reluctant to invest in such states even if the country is politically and economically stable.

Rijckeghem and Weder (2001) did what they considered the first empirical estimate of the effects of pay in the civil service on corruption. This study tested whether there is a systematic relationship between wages in the civil service and corruption both across countries over time. A wage variable choice, comparing the ratio of government wages to manufacturing wages, was used. Data used were from the IMF, statistical yearbooks, central bank bulletins, and the International Labor Organization (ILO) yearbooks. For relative wages, data were gathered from Rauch and Evans (2000). Data on corruption were also gathered from the ICRG. Several proxies of the probability of detection were used for quality of the bureaucracy. The authors found a loose negative association between relative civil service wages and corruption across the developing and lower-income Organization for Economic Cooperation and Development (OECD) countries.

Some studies have focused on gender and corruption. The presence of women has become vital in African politics where previously they were considered unwelcome. The increase in women in today's governing might partly be credited to studies showing that women are less likely to condone corruption and thereby less involved in bribery. In their study on gender and corruption, Swamy et al. (2001) ascertained that in hypothetical situations, women are less likely to overlook corruption. Further, they suggested that those countries that have greater representation of women in government or in the private sector also have lower levels of corruption. They drew on the World Values Survey (Inglehart et al. 1998) in which men and women in a large number of developed and developing countries were questioned about their ethical attitudes in a range of hypothetical situations. Using a Likert Scale questionnaire, they asked 12 questions about ethical choices, with a scale where 1 was "bribery is never justified," to 10, "bribery can always be justified." Respondents were confronted with choices like claiming government benefits to which they were not entitled, cheating on taxes if one seems to have the chance to get away with it, buying something known to be stolen, lying in one's own interest, accepting a bribe in the course of their duties, and so on. They also used data from an unpublished World Bank study of corruption in the country of Georgia, which included a survey of 350 firms. The result of this study indicated that, at least in the short or medium term, increased presence of women in public life could reduce levels of corruption. They cautioned that this is not a claim that corruptibility is a biological trait but that the gender differences they observed may be attributed to socialization, or to differences in access to networks of corruption, or in knowledge of how to engage in corrupt practices, or to other factors. The study found that the percentage of women who say corruption is "never justified" is higher than the percentage of men who give the same response. They argued that greater participation by women in public life should have a greater impact on corruption in countries in which the gender gap is larger.

Two examples of women's transparent leadership in the Africa of today are Ellen Johnson Sirleaf, President of Liberia, and Joyce Banda, President of Malawi. Sirleaf was awarded the 2011 Noble Peace Prize and recognized for her non-violent struggle for the safety of women. Joyce Banda told the *Johannesburg Telegraph* during a visit to South Africa:

> When I took over, the economy had almost collapsed. I told Malawians we needed to pass through difficult times. I even cut my own salary by 30 percent to show we are making sacrifices. It is a very low salary, but most Malawians are getting just as little as that. (as cited in Laing 2012, p. 1)

That was an unprecedented action by any African leader. Nevertheless, as the Nigerian media regularly reveals, Nigerian women leaders are not immune to corruption. In the years since they first became engaged in roles such as heads of government establishments, legislators, ministers, and other positions of powers, women leaders have often been accused of money laundering and stealing from the public budgets they are responsible for (e.g., Madu 2013). Although this single media article is not a compelling source, and the focus on women can be misleading in terms of corruption frequency compared to men, the report does give an impression of the range of possibilities by which corruption can happen in everyday life among female representatives of the elite (Madu 2013; Sampson and Decker 2010).

Manifestations of Corruption: Different Sectors, Different Agents

One of the most intensive comparative studies on corruption in Africa was conducted by French anthropologists Giorgio Blundo and Jean-Pierre Oliver de Sardan in Benin, Niger and Senegal. They developed a useful typology of forms of corruption that maps well unto the Nigerian scene. The seven basic forms they identified, as summarized and annotated by Smith (2006), are:

> (1) commission for illicit services: "payment by users to officials who then grant access to unwarranted advantages... (2) unwarranted payment for public services... an official forcing a user to pay for service that is ostensibly provided for free, or inflating the cost of a routine service... (3) gratuities... payment for services after the fact, and commonly couched in the idiom of a "thank you"... (4) string-pulling... using social

and political influence to promote favoritism...(5) levies and tolls...stark forms of tribute that persons in a position of power can extract from ordinary citizens...(6) sidelining...use of public or company resources for private purposes...(and) (7) Misappropriation...public materials not only used for private purposes, but expropriated entirely...(Smith 2006, p. 17).

Thus, corruption manifests itself in many forms. Cullen (2008) summarized these into three categories according to the sector where they are practiced, political, bureaucratic, and business corruptions, which is in line with Ksenia's (2008) three categories of corruption: bureaucratic, political, and grand.

Political corruption is characterized by grand or big-ticket corruption conducted by political elites, explained Cullen (2008). These leaders use their position to salt away money from their countries, money they acquired from bribery and corruption. Transparency International (2004) named the ten most corrupt national leaders and revealed that four of them stole 5–10 billion dollars each. Two of the leaders are from Africa. Cullen summarized the total money siphoned by the ten leaders to grotesque numbers of a low of $32 billion to a high of $58 billion. He imagined how many hospitals this could have built, how many schools, or how much food could have been purchased to alleviate hunger and starvation around the globe.

Cullen (2008) classified bureaucratic corruption as that practiced by state functionaries. It is usually a matter of petty bribery and corruption at the middle management and junior levels of government. Often it is an encouragement to "supplement" low wages and salaries, a practice dating back to the colonial era. In the novel, *Mister Johnson (n.d.)*, set in colonial Nigeria, Joyce Cary in 1939 depicted a native clerk who regularly steals from his European employer to support his lifestyle. Eventually this leads to a tragic end, but along the way, the title character effectively manages projects serving his masters' colonial purposes. To this day, at the local, state, and national government levels in Nigeria, one can hardly get any projects, large or small, done without bribing officials from the lowest to the highest levels.

Business corruption is primarily limited to a smaller and more defined group of stakeholders—shareholders, workers, management, and potentially suppliers and customers, claimed Cullen. Those who offer or give bribes to secure contracts are just as much the problem as the takers of bribes.

Researchers in this field regularly cite the works of Paolo Mauro as he is regarded as one of the frontrunners in the study of corruption. Mauro (1995) studied how corruption affects investment and growth for a cross section of about 70 countries, utilizing the Business International Indices of Corruption (BI), which is now incorporated into The Economist Intelligent Unit. He utilized nine indicators of institutional efficiency as defined by BI: political change (institutional), political stability (social), probability of opposition group takeover, stability of labor, relationship with neighboring countries, terrorism, legal system (judiciary), bureaucracy and red tape, and corruption. He chose these nine factors for two reasons: "First they are assessed independently of macro-economic variables; second, they refer to the interests of any firm operating in the country in question, rather than specifically to foreign-owned multi national companies" (Mauro 1995, p. 690). He noted that all BI indices are positively and significantly correlated. The author found that corruption is strongly and negatively associated with the investment rate, regardless of the amount of red tape. Institutional inefficiency causes low investment. The null hypothesis of no relationship between investment and corruption can be rejected at a level of significance higher than the null hypothesis of no relationship between growth and corruption.

Mo (2001) made use of the Transparency International Corruption Perception Index and the panel data set assembled by Robert Barro and Jong-Wha Lee. The author described the study as a new perspective on the role of corruption in economic growth and explained that it provides quantitative estimates of the impact of corruption on the growth and importance of the transmission channels. Acknowledging that the corruption variable is defined as the degree to which business transactions involve corruption and questionable payment, Mo claimed that the exact channels through which corruption affects economic growth are not resolved empirically. He therefore developed a new analytical framework to estimate the effects of corruption and the channels through which it affects the rate of GDP growth. He used investment, human capital, and political instability as channels to estimate the effects of corruption. Mo concluded that the most important channel through which corruption affects economic growth is political instability, which accounts for about 53 % of the overall effect, while investment and human capital share the remaining percentage.

Blackburn et al. (2010) presented an analysis of the joint determination of bureaucratic corruption and economic development based on a simple model of growth in which bureaucrats are employed as agents of government to collect taxes from households. The study relied on corruption perception indices with data sets constructed on the basis of questionnaire surveys sent to a network of correspondents around the world. The authors acknowledged that good quality governance is essential for sustained economic development and that corruption in the public sector is a major impediment to growth and prosperity. However, they opined that despite a large body of evidence to support the theory, there remains relatively little formal theoretical analysis that would lend rigor and precision to the argument involved. While recognizing that there are other factors besides economic considerations that may affect corruption in different countries, they concluded that corruption remains highly significant and is undoubtedly a major determinant in economic development.

Zhao et al. (2003) studied the impact of corruption and transparency on Foreign Direct Investment (FDI). They expressed the need for a close and systematic examination of the actual and specific effects corruption and transparency may have on FDI, accounting for other crucial factors. After an extensive review of literature on the effects of corruption on FDI, they developed two hypotheses: "*Hypothesis 1*: Other factors being equal, corruption is likely to lead to a reduced FDI. The higher the corruption level, the lower the level of DFI inflow... *Hypothesis 2:* The presence of low transparency in a host country is likely to hinder the inflow of FDI to that country. The lower the transparency, the lower the level of inward FDI" (pp. 46–47).

Based on these hypotheses, the authors developed a model incorporating a number of business environment variables in relation to the impacts of corruption. Panel data on corruption from Transparency International were used as well as FDI/GDP data from annual International Financial Statistics of the International Monetary Fund. Based on their findings Zhao, Kim, and Du call upon policy-makers to "fight on two fronts" (p. 59), one of these being "that the public as well as governments" (p. 59) must be engaged in the enhancement of transparency and fighting corruption. This brings us to the main argument I make based on a lifetime of work at home and abroad on Nigeria's entrenched, multi-level corruption.

How to Counter and Prevent Corruption (Government and Civil Society)

The fight against corruption is incumbent on good governance. It is important in the public sector, the private sector, and the not-for-profit sector. The culture of corruption is exacerbated when any one of these sectors has weak governance (Cullen 2008). Corruption has to do with the degree of democracy and development in countries, and both are factors in countering corruption. In exploring two broad reasons why corruption may be costly to economic development, Shleifer and Vishny (1993) explained that weak central government that allows various governmental agencies and bureaucracies to impose independent bribes on private agents are cutting short their source of revenue. They also opined that the distortion entailed by the necessary secrecy of corruption can shift a country's investments away from the highest value projects. They argued that these two factors explained why corruption is so high in some less developed countries and so costly to development.

The United Nations Convention against Corruption (United Nations Office on Drugs and Crime 2004) identified and agreed upon good governance and other means for combating corruption. These included measures for prevention, criminalization, international cooperation, and asset recovery. One hundred forty countries concurred that while corruption can be prosecuted after the fact, first and foremost, fighting it requires prevention. Several different articles of the Convention are dedicated to prevention, with measures directed at both the public and private sectors. These include model preventive policies, such as the establishment of anti-corruption bodies and enhanced transparency in the financing of election campaigns and political parties. The Convention requires countries to establish criminal and other offences to cover a wide range of acts of corruption if these are not already crimes under domestic law. The Convention goes beyond previous instruments of this kind, not only criminalizing basic forms of corruption but also calling for a reaffirmation of core values of honesty, accountability, and transparency. Bear this priority of the Convention in mind as I come to a detailed account of oath taking. In the Convention, nations are also encouraged to cooperate with one another in every aspect of the fight against corruption, including prevention, investigation, and the prosecution of offenders. Nations are bound by the convention to render specific forms of mutual legal assistance in gathering and transferring evidence for use in court. In a major breakthrough, countries agreed on asset recovery, which is stated explicitly as a fundamental principle of the convention. This is a particularly important issue for many developing countries where high-level corruption has plundered the national wealth, and where resources are badly needed for reconstruction and the rehabilitation of societies.

Coker et al. (2012) made important recommendations on how to combat and prevent corruption in their paper on the challenges of implementing anti-corruption programs under Nigeria's president Obasanjo from 1999 to 2007. They suggested that:

> The Act enacting anti-corruption agencies should clearly demonstrate the multifarious nature of corruption and other related offences and appropriate sanctions provided; the immunity granted certain public officers should be removed in order to discourage corrupt practices and other related vices by public office holders; the Customs, Police and Immigration departments should be overhauled, and corrupt officials relieved of their duties; collaborations by multinational corporations/government and indigenous agents should be severely penalized; and, Foreign governments and international financial institutions should assist Nigeria locate and repatriate looted monies from the country by the past and present public officers. (p. 79)

The recommendations are solidly in line with the views of United Nations Secretary General Kofi Annan: "Addressing the problem of corruption would require targeting both payer and recipient" (as quoted in Van Vuuren 2002, p. 67).

Hanlon et al. (2000) urged rich lending countries and agencies to restore some justice to a system in which international creditors play the role of plaintiff, judge, and jury in their own court of international finance. They encouraged such bodies to introduce discipline into sovereign lending and borrowing arrangements—and thereby prevent future crises. This way they will be able to counter corruption in borrowing and lending by introducing accountability through a free press and greater transparency to civil society in both the creditor and debtor nations. Hanlon et al. claimed this approach will strengthen local democratic institutions by empowering them to challenge and influence elites thereby encouraging greater understanding and economic literacy among citizens and empowering them to question, challenge, and hold their elites to account.

Many countries now have anti-corruption commissions and laws guiding against corruption. But the impact is disappointing. In Indonesia, under the Habibie administration in the late 1990s, Law 31/99 on corruption created special provisions for investigating corrupt acts by public officials and provided for the establishment of an anti-corruption commission. According to Sherlock (2002), Law 28/99 created the KPKPN (Komisi Pemeriksa Kekayaan Penyelenggara Negara)—the Commission to Audit the Wealth of State Officials, or, for short, the Assets Auditing Commission. Also, a presidential decree in 2000 by Abdurrahman Wahid created a National Ombudsman's Commission (Komisi Ombudsman National, KON). Yet, Indonesia is still high on the corrupt countries list.

While the establishment of anti-corruption commissions may not have a great impact on corruption in some countries despite the prosecution and sentencing of offenders, Ying (2004) reported that the establishment of anti-corruption commissions has yielded dividends in other countries. In his study, he explored the successes and failures of corruption control strategies employed by three non-democratic regimes in the post-World War II era. The establishment of the Corruption Practices Investigation Bureau (CPIB) in Singapore is one of the reasons why that nation is rated very high among the non-corrupt nations. Similarly, in Hong Kong the Independent Commission against Corruption (ICAC) has been an effective watchdog that keeps the nation clean.

The United Nations Office of Drug and Crime (UNODC) has established relations with civil society around the world in the war on corruption. Its fight against corruption includes prevention and criminal justice, drug prevention, treatment and care, drug trafficking, firearms, fraudulent medicines, HIV and AIDS, human trafficking and migrant smuggling, money laundering, organized crime, piracy, terrorism, and wildlife and forest crime. The UNODC has emphasized that the role of civil society and the media in the fight against corruption not only consists of denouncing acts of corruption, but also increasingly in concrete collaboration with national governments, regional groups, and the private sector. Through the framework of the UNCAC, UNODC is working with over 100 NGOs from across the world, equipping them with the tools they need to work constructively with governments and the public. In Ghana, for example, UNODC is working with an anti-corruption NGO that has created a Network of Journalist Against Corruption. The aim of the network is to build journalists' capacity to improve investigative reporting. The Ghana Anti-Corruption Coalition has also launched a platform for regional businesses to obtain and share information on their business code and anti-corruption policies. Not only does this platform aim to create awareness on anti-corruption policies in the business sector, it also offers the possibility of signing integrity pacts with public institutions to provide services and develop principles by which they will then abide (Ghana Anti-Corruption n.d.).

The Association of Nigerians against Corruption (ANAC), the civic organization that has been the motor for this book, falls in the same category of NGO initiatives. The intervention I focus on, oath taking, has involved the commitment of hundreds of people over the years. Their decision to take a voluntary oath against corruption must have been guided by certain principles that include motivation, morality, and ethics, among others.

Motivation: What It Means and Why Do People Get Involved in Civil Action?

ANAC's efforts cannot be successful if the civil society is not motivated to be part of the anti-corruption vanguard. For the initiatives in both Nigeria and Dayton, Ohio, it is critically necessary to understand what motivated the participants to take a voluntary public oath against corruption and commit to living by that for the rest of their lives.

Landy and Becker (1987) wrote that reviews about the concept of *motivation* have unearthed some 140 distinct definitions. The term is from the Latin word *motus*, which also forms the verb *movere*, to move. By motivation we mean the degree to which a person is moved or aroused to expend effort to achieve some purpose (Steers and Porter 1987).

Bauer and Erdogen (2009) defined motivation as "the desire to achieve a goal or certain performance level" (p. 560). According to Dawson (as cited in Thompson and McHugh 2002), motivation can drive someone to act to achieve his or her goal. It is something internal that leads to behavior. A motivated person will be more likely to perform maximum capacity in their job.

Organizations have benefitted from applying motivation theories to energize employees and foster a stimulating work environment. These theories are categorized as either content or process theories. Bauer and Erdogen (2009) explained that many organizations have applied motivation theories, such as goal-setting theory and reinforcement theory, in order to modify their employees' behavior in the workplace through goals and reward systems. According to the reinforcement theory of Bauer and Erdogen, behavior that is rewarded is often repeated. As a result, many organizations have utilized this theory by tying rewards to performance. In the case of oath taking, urging interventions against corruption in everyday life, the response might be retaliation rather than external rewards. This makes the impact of "rewards" less straightforward, and probably more a question of internal rewards. The study seeks to shed light on these and other meanings of "reward" in the case of everyday interventions against corruption.

The participants in the study are not employees of an organization getting monetary reward for taking and keeping the oath. They are individuals who agreed to join the Association of Nigerians against Corruption by publicly taking an oath against corruption. For them there must be a sense of purpose, for instance, a relation to their sense of self-worth or capability to achieve something, rather than the pursuit of money. According to Rainey (2001), a person may gain motivation by feeling a greater ability to perform or have motivation diminished by frustration because of inadequate ability to perform well. This brings us to Maslow's classical theory.

Maslow's Theory of Motivation

A discussion of motivation can hardly ignore Maslow's seminal work on motivation (Maslow 1943). Maslow's Hierarchy of Needs theory as shown in Fig. 2.1 and Herzberg's Motivation-Hygiene Theory (Frederick Herzberg motivational theory, n.d.) are important and popular theories within content motivation. Maslow's "Hierarchy of Needs" theory is divided into five levels and arranged in ascending order according to human needs: physiological needs, safety needs, social needs, esteem needs, and self-actualization needs (Adler 1977). Among the five levels, the hierarchical needs can be divided into two groups: lower order needs and higher order needs (Wood et al. 2006). Lower order needs consist of physiological, safety, and social needs, while the high order needs consist of esteem and self-actualization needs.

All of these are essential needs in the Nigeria of today. The breakdown of law and order has led to constant raids of armed robbers in several communities. Armed robbers operate at will on highways although the police and army constantly mount checkpoints.

The lowest level, physiological needs, was believed to be the most basic of all. Physiological needs contain elements such as air, food, and water. Though air is a given need from nature, the air in many of the big cities is highly polluted from the fumes of unregulated automobile and motorcycle

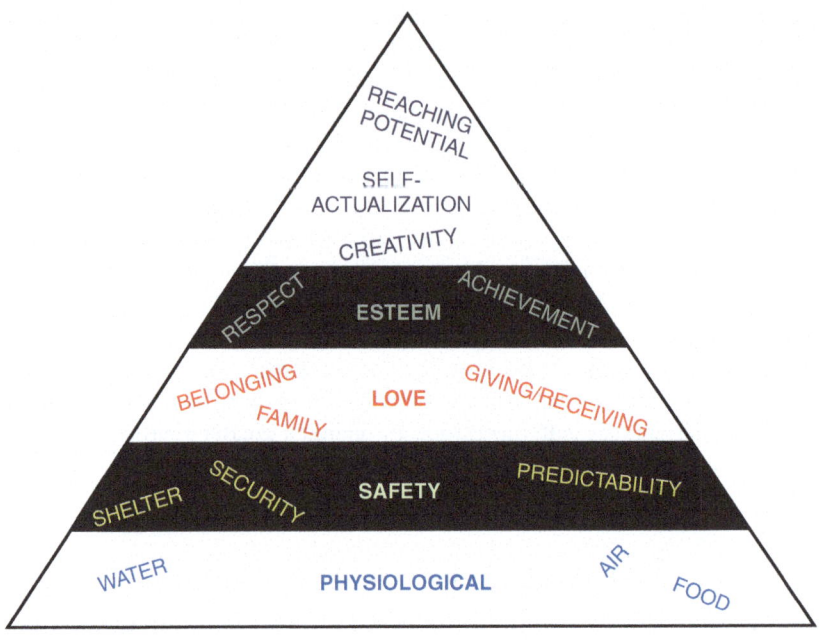

Fig. 2.1 Maslow's hierarchy of needs theory. Based on ideas of Maslow (1943)

(okada) emissions. Pipe-borne water, which used to be supplied by local governments for various communities, is no more in existence. People now rely on boreholes or flowing streams for their water needs. The second level is safety needs, such as protection from dangerous threats and stability in daily life (Wood et al. 2006). The terror of Boko Haram (the Islamic insurgency militant group, see Onuoha 2010) has put the nation in a state of ceaseless unrest, creating an environment where this second level of need for safety is in continual jeopardy.

Mazlow's third level is about social needs such as for family, friends, love, and affection. The needs for self-esteem follow. This is a need for acceptance and recognition by others. The highest level of the hierarchical pyramid is the self-actualization need. This is what an individual does to achieve their wishes. Morality, which is housed in this part of the pyramid, is also part of safety at the second level of the pyramid.

What motivated the oath takers who became participants in this study to take a voluntary oath against corruption may have been governed by needs at every level of the pyramid as those needs may have been inadequately supplied in the society as a result of pervasive corruption. However, the morality aspect of the pyramid stands out as an internal motivation, thus making morality and ethics relevant to this study.

Maslow's theory justifies needs for civil action, as promoted by ANAC through the use of God-centered approach of oath taking. The Bible confirmed the need for individuals to abstain from corruption when Jesus spoke to his disciples on the source of corruption:

> What comes out of a person is what defiles them. For it is from within, out of a person's heart, that evil thoughts come—sexual immorality, theft, murder, adultery, greed, malice, deceit, lewdness, envy, slander, arrogance and folly. All these evils come from inside and define a person. (7 Mark: 20–22, New International Version)

Several researchers have proposed modifications to Maslow's theory. Barnes (1960) proposed a two-step hierarchy consisting of physiological needs at the base and a higher level made up of self-esteem, esteem of others, and belongingness. Harrison (1966) and Hall and Nougaim (1968) argued against Maslow's theory. Harrison offered a modification model in which physiological-economic needs were at the base. He concluded that upon satisfaction of these needs, a higher level of social or ego satisfaction would be sought. Hall and Nougaim designed a longitudinal study to test key propositions in the Maslow theory. They reported some difficulty developing operational definitions for the Maslow system, and their results provided almost no support for the Maslow theory.

Alderfer (1969) tested an alternative theory based on a three-fold conceptualization of human needs: existence, relatedness, and growth (E.R.G.) dealing with the problem of how need satisfaction was related to need strength.

Heylighen (1992) criticized the needs hierarchy and model of self-actualizing personality in his cognitive-systematic reconstruction of Maslow's theory, asserting that the definition of self-actualization is confusing and the gratification of all needs is insufficient to explain self-actualization. He described self-actualizers as people who have the patience to endure the things that cannot be changed and wisdom to distinguish the ones from the others. On self-actualizers' relations with other people, society, and culture, Heylighen claimed this is characterized by their autonomy. "They do not really need other people," he wrote, continuing:

> They make their decisions for themselves without having to rely on the opinions of others, or on the rules, conventions and values imposed by society. They like solitude and detachment, and have a need for privacy and independence. Their world view is generally independent of the particular culture or society in which they live, and they pay little attention to the social conventions, though they will superficially respect them if transgressing the rules would bring about needless conflicts. (p. 43)

Heylighen's contention is more Western than African oriented and departs from the idea of community culture in Africa where the individual exists primarily in relation to the community, its norms and culture. Such cultures can bind the community to the extent that some might risk their lives, based upon some ethics and morals, for the good of the community. At the same time, people who take the oath go against today's community culture that accepts bribery and puts them in a position of the autonomous moral agent, as many revolutionary leaders have been autonomous moral agents, such as Jesus Christ, Gandhi, Mandela, or Mohammed. It is the courage to take that position that can be related to oath takers who know they might be shunned by the community for refusing to conform.

Ethics and morals for the good of the community can be related to Mayer et al.'s (2013) study of conditions that encourage whistle blowing. Mayer et al. showed that social environments play a major role when it comes to reporting unethical conduct: "It takes a village to get employees to internally report misconduct" (p. 89). Of course, to even think of reporting unethical conduct one must be against it and willing to take risks, as participants in the study for this book have done. At the same time, an oath against bribery also places the individual in a relatively autonomous choice position against community convention to offer and take bribes. The oath fulfills a sense of moral obligation, not a community requirement as will be discussed below in considering individual morality. It can be theorized that the choice that the oath takers make in the corrupt environment can transform the decision of the perpetrators for good or bad.

In their book *Courageous Resistance: The Power of Ordinary People,* Thalhammer et al. (2007) stated that a good choice in a dangerous situation can sometimes prevent abuses of power or save some lives otherwise destined for destruction. A good choice is a motivating factor for courageous resisters. Thalhammer and her colleagues contended that certain preconditions and external factors heighten the likelihood of people becoming courageous resisters. These are socializing, reinforcing, and modeling learning by doing. Others involve attitude toward authority, helping others, and in-group and out-group identification. The more inclusive the in-group is in terms of crossing boundaries, the more one will be inclined to intervene against injustice. Networks and context were considered external factors such as friends, organizations, social values, domestic and international climate, transitional advocacy networks, and institutions and rules. These networks can provide an environment more or less supportive of honoring justice for all. Thalhammer et al. outline one of the few theories of what it takes for ordinary people to choose for acting against, rather than complying with injustice. What they labeled as a "process of perceiving and responding to injustice" leads toward three classifications of people: perpetrators, bystanders, and resisters.

In my study, I apply the meaning of perpetrators from Thalhammer et al. (2007, pp. 4–5) as individuals, collectives, or institutions whose actions and policies result in the serious mistreatment of a person or group of persons. Bystanders are those who are neither the direct perpetrators of unjust acts nor the victims and who also do not engage in active resistance to such actions. Resisters are defined as those who voluntarily and consciously decide to engage in other-oriented, largely selfless behavior with a significant high risk or cost to themselves or their associates.

Thalhammer et al. (2007) stated that a person can become a perpetrator or bystander because of several dimensions of the context of a situation—social, cultural, religious, political, or economic dimensions, for example. Corruption as an act of injustice has no boundary. At the time of the study for this book, a group of Islamic radicals, Boko Haram, holds a section of Nigeria as ransom to propagate their beliefs. They have seized young college girls and killed several people in gun and bomb attacks. There have been allegations from several media outlets that the group is sponsored by politicians and that the police and army are in the pay roll of the organization. If so, it would be but the most extreme consequence of countless examples of how corruption in Nigeria destroys the nation. Even if not true, that such allegations seem at all possible indicates the seriousness of our country's situation.

Usually, bystanders are considered passive supporters of the perpetrators. The role of unconcerned bystanders is essential in perpetuating corruption. "Perpetrators and their peers often interpret bystanders' inactive as tacit support for their malevolent actions" (Thalhammer et al. 2007, p. 40). The participants in this study are adults who in the course of their life have been socialized by family, at school, in the mosque or church, which could have some bearing on their life. Living in a society where corruption is the order of the day, the attitudes of the participants toward authority could be positive or negative depending on the examples they have been exposed to during their formative years. Were they perpetrators, passive bystanders, or resisters before taking the oath, and what happened after they took the oath? Thalhammer et al. (2007) wrote that whether a person becomes a courageous resister depends on how he or she reacts upon becoming aware of grave injustice. Were the participants in the study aware of any unjust practice before they took the oath or after? People must decide whether to courageously resist the injustice, stand by and do nothing while it occurs, or intentionally participate in the unjust activity.

Ethics and Moral Principles as Motivating Factors

Connolly et al. (2009) described ethics as the "philosophical study of morality" (p. 11) with both words being used synonymously. They defined morality as the behavior of making value judgments regarding how we should best live our lives.

Velasquez (2002) defined ethics as, "the discipline that examines one's moral standards or the moral standards of a society" (p. 15). However, ethics as a discipline is something different from the ethics that guide our life in the same way that medicine as a discipline is something different from the practice of medicine, even though related. Who or what determines the ethical standard? Velasquez et al. (2010) further explain: "First, ethics refers to well-founded standards of right and wrong that prescribe what humans ought to do, usually in terms of rights, obligations, benefits to society, fairness, or specific virtues" (p. 10). Ethics therefore are shared values, part of a group, and part of a culture. Ethics, for example, refers to those standards that impose the reasonable obligations to refrain from rape, stealing, murder, assault, slander, and fraud. Ethical standards also include those that enjoin the virtues of honesty, compassion, and loyalty. Ethical standards include standards relating to rights, such as the right to life, the right to freedom from injury, and the right to privacy. Such standards are adequate standards of ethics because they are supported by consistent and well-founded reasons. Second, ethics refers to the study and development of one's ethical standards. Feelings, laws, and social norms can deviate from what is ethical. Questions can be raised as to who decides what is ethical. What if the majority of police on the road blocks in Nigeria finds it normal to take bribes as they do? Who decides then that it is unethical? So it is necessary to constantly examine one's standards to ensure that they are reasonable and well founded. Ethics also means, then, the continuous effort of scrutinizing our own moral beliefs and our moral conduct and striving to ensure that we, and the institutions we help to shape, live up to standards that are reasonable and solidly based.

Velasquez (2002) explained:

> A person begins to do ethics when he or she turns to look at the moral standards that have been absorbed from family, church, friends, and society, and begins asking whether these standards are reasonable or unreasonable and what these standards imply for situations and issues. (p. 12)

Moral standards are a key factor in the determination of ethical behavior. It is therefore necessary to have a clear understanding of the term. According to Velasquez (2002), "moral reasoning refers to the reasoning process by which human behaviors, institutions, or policies are judged to be in accordance with or in violation of moral standards" (p. 33). It involves two essential components:

1. An understanding of what reasonable moral standards require, prohibit, value, or condemn and evidence or information that shows that a particular person, policy, institution, or behavior has the kinds of features that these moral standards require, prohibit, value, or condemn;
2. Moral reasoning must be logical. The analysis of moral reasoning requires that the logic of the arguments used to establish a moral judgment must be rigorously examined. Second, the factual evidence cited to support individual judgment must be accurate,

relevant, and complete. Third, the moral standards involved in a person's moral reasoning must be consistent.

How did participants in the study talk about ethical behavior or messages received during childhood through the influence of family, friends, and church or mosque in relation to anti-corruption? What were the ambivalences and dilemmas they faced, if any, in living up consistently to their moral judgment? Answers to these and other questions emerged from their life stories as examined here.

Development of Ethics/Moral Standards

"Morality claims our lives," according to Thiroux and Krasemann (1977, p. 1). They explained that morality makes claims upon each of us that are stronger than the claims of law and take priority over self-interest. They defined morality as dealing basically with humans and how they relate to other beings, both human and nonhuman. Four aspects of morality were considered vital by Thiroux and Krasemann:

> *Religious Morality* refers to a human being in relationship to a supernatural being or beings; *Morality and Nature*... refers to a human being in relationship to nature... (as) prevalent in primitive culture; *Individual morality* refers to individuals in relation to themselves and to an individual code of morality that may or may not be sanctioned by any society or religion... (and) social morality (which)concerns a human being in relation to other human beings. It is probably the most important aspect of morality, in that it cuts across all of the other aspects and is found in more ethical systems than any of the others. (pp. 9–10, italics added)

Shermer (2004) explained that the study of morality is the study of why humans do what we do particularly on the social level, since all moral issues revolve around how we interact with others. He claimed that morality involves issues of right and wrong thoughts and behavior, while ethics involves the study of right and wrong thought and behavior as applicable to rules and conducts. He traced moral sentiments and concomitant behaviors to human evolution over hundreds of thousands of years. In this sense, moral sentiments and behaviors exist beyond us; we simply inherit them, fine tune, and tweak them according to our cultural and personal preferences, and apply them within our unique historical circumstances. This would explain the variety of moral behavior between and within cultures, including in Nigeria.

Haidt (2012) built on Shermer's theory by blending his research findings with those of anthropologists, historians, and psychologists. Answering the question of where morality comes from, he revealed: nature and nurture. Nativists believe that moral knowledge is native in our minds and comes preloaded, perhaps in our God-inscribed hearts (as the Bible says) or in our evolved moral emotions (as Darwinians argue). If you believe that children are more or less a blank slate at birth (as John Locke's philosophy did), then one is an empiricist. Haidt rejected the third approach by Jean Piaget claiming rationalism, in which children figure out morality for themselves based on their experience with harm. Singer (2000) further clarified the concept of ethics by writing that the universal aspect of ethics provides a persuasive, although not conclusive reason for taking a broadly utilitarian position.

> If we are to accept that a person is living according to ethical standards, the justification must be of a certain kind. For instance, a justification in terms of self-interest alone will not do. Self-interested acts must be shown to be compatible with more broadly based ethical principles if they are to be ethically defensible, for the notion of ethics carries with it the idea of something bigger than the individual. (p. 14)

Singer (2000) argued that reasons play an important role in ethical decisions. He raised questions about what is it to live according to ethical standards or make a moral judgment. He argued that if a person is living according to ethical standards, the justification must be of a certain kind. Self-interested acts must be shown to be compatible with more broadly based ethical principles. Singer concluded that the notion of ethics carries with it the idea of something bigger than the individual. He reflected on those who lie and cheat, but do not believe that what they do is wrong, and may be living too according to ethical standards. He argued that for a number of reasons some may believe that it is right to lie, cheat, steal, and so on.

The three categories of ethical and moral justification, understanding moral standards, logical moral reasoning, and consistency in moral action, could hold explanations for the participants of this study to take a public oath against corruption. These might emerge from their life history.

OATH AND RELIGION

Oath taking is one way that people try to live up to their ethics and moral standards. The American Heritage College Dictionary (1993) defined an oath as a "solemn formal declaration or promise, often calling on God, or a sacred object as witness" (p. 939). According to Garlington (1995),

> An "oath" or "vow" as used in the Hebrew Scriptures, may be called "a sworn affirmation or an invocation of God in affirmation of a promise. It is a solemn appeal to God to confirm the truth of one's words, with the express acceptance of punishment in case one fails to speak the truth. (p. 6)

From time immemorial, oaths have been used to formally and legally make a pledge, one that should be binding and, with the invocation of God or any other deity, considered sacred to the individual or personality. The administration of an oath is a very serious business, and it is usually accompanied with a formal swearing-in ceremony. Both the oath and swearing-in of a personage to public office connote a sacred process and a public utterance of a sacred obligation to the yearning and aspiration of the people involved.

Oaths in themselves do not hold any legal obligations, unless as part of the swearing-in for public service positions. But they are commonly taken despite not being an enforceable guarantee morality. Nevertheless, people take oaths all over the world. Presidents of countries around the globe take an oath before assuming offices. Senators, congressmen, judges, and other government officials take oaths. New citizens of various countries take a naturalization oath. Many schoolchildren take an oath or pledge allegiance to the flag of their countries. Plaintiffs and defendants raise their hands and take the oath in court hearings. Professionals such as doctors, military, and police take an oath before assuming duties. As we have seen from the many examples I discussed where government officials violate ethics by taking bribes, an oath is no guarantee against corruption. It is a moral reminder that the person commits to virtues such as honesty and truth telling.

According to Ricks (1999),

> The well-being and security of a community depend on its members speaking the truth in matters of crucial importance. Oaths provide a means of impressing on those party to such a matter their obligation to truthfulness

and dependability, while at the same time increasing the oath takers' seriousness and credibility in the eyes of others. (p. 2)

Oath taking is considered a sworn affirmation to something, such as one's belief, religion, or a symbolic representation. Given the fact that the large majority of Nigerians are religious (Awolalu 1976), it is relevant to pay attention to religion as a possible inspiration for oath taking against corruption.

Velasquez et al. (2010) stated that no one should identify ethics with religion. They claimed most religions advocate high ethical standards, yet acting ethically is not restricted to deeply religious people. Ethics applies as much to the behavior of the atheist as to that of the devout. Religion can set high ethical standards and can provide intense motivations for ethical behavior. In their book *Ethics Without God*, Nielsen and Moreland (1990) equated the breakdown of ethical morality to the decline of Christianity: "The roots of the horror of the twentieth century, lie in the breakdown of an absolutistic Christian morality" (p. 77). But to correlate ethical acts with piety in Christianity is to forget about the inquisition and about the plunder, massacre, and enslavement of so much of the world in the name of Christ. Nielsen and Moreland argued that without religion we would scarcely be human beings and that without God men and women will quickly become subhuman. Ethics, however, cannot be confined to religion, nor is it the same as religion.

The relation between oath taking and religion goes far back into history. In the Hebrew Scriptures the taking of an oath is considered a sworn affirmation or an invocation of God in confirmation of a promise. It is considered a solemn appeal to God to confirm the truth of one's words, with the express acceptance of punishment in case one fails to speak the truth.

In his treatise *On Christian Doctrine*, John Milton (as cited in Lewis 1835) described the oath as "that whereby we call God to witness the truth of what we say, with a curse upon ourselves ... should it prove false" (Lewis 1835, p. 4). Ricks (1999) drew on John Milton's treatise *On Christian Doctrine* to identify "three major elements of the oath in the Old Testament:

(1) the *oath statement*, in which the swearer asserts that he has or has not done something or in which he promises that he will or will not do something; (2) the *witness invocation*, in which God or some other person, being, or object is called on to witness the words of the oath and, by implication, to

act as an accuser if the oath is not fulfilled; and, (3) the *curse formula*, which is either explicitly stated or implied by some bodily gesture. (p. 49)."

In the Jewish religious mind, an oath is an appeal to God to witness matters in dispute and calling him as a witness to a lie is the height of profanity. Oath taking took the form of a self-curse if the condition was not fulfilled. According to Garlington (1995), oath keeping is essential for society as it is the base of its security. People are expected to keep their promises in matters of serious import. He classified oaths into three categories: an exculpatory oath for defendants to back their pleas of innocence in the absence of witnesses; the adjuration, when giving testimony; and the voluntary obligatory oath.

For this study, a voluntary oath is most relevant. All oaths, especially when voluntary, "had to be fulfilled even at the risk of harm to oneself" (Garlington 1995, p. 20). Oath taking does have its critics. According to Garlington some think it only encourages self-importance and fuels paternalism, and others see it as a bid for respectability: the church, the bar in law, and the armed forces all swear oaths. Garlington also pointed out that there are those who think oath taking is discouraged in the Bible by quoting Jesus in Matthew 5:33–37 (New International Version):

> Again you have heard that it was said to the people long ago: Do not break your oath, but fulfill to the Lord the vows you have made. But I tell you, do not swear an oath at all: either by heaven, for it is God's throne; (35) or by the earth, for it is his footstool; or by Jerusalem, for it is the city of the Great King. And do not swear by your head, for you cannot make even one hair white or black. All you need to say is simply Yes or No; anything beyond this come from the evil one.

This passage does not condemn oath taking as it begins urging not to break oaths by fulfilling to the Lord the vows made. But critics point out that Jesus also advised not to swear an oath at all; hence, they say oaths should be abolished. Clarity is often hard to achieve when drawing on the Bible for guidance on whether or not to take oaths.

Africa: Religion and Oath Taking

Given the importance of religion to many Nigerians my research must look at the role of religion as a motivating factor of taking or living up to the oath. According to Adeniyi (2001), it is imperative that religion plays an important role in combating ubiquitous acts of corruption. He suggested that religion dictates to its followers basic values intended to guide them toward living an ideal lifestyle and would be a good weapon to fight corruption if its values are appropriately applied.

Religion is fundamental and important in African cultures. In order to understand religion in Africa one has to first look at it from the standpoint of traditional faiths in Africa. Awolalu (1976) explained:

> When we speak of African Traditional Religion, we mean the indigenous religious belief and practices of the Africans. It is the religion which resulted from the sustaining faith held by the forbears of the present Africans, and which is being practiced today in various forms and various shades and intensities by a very large number of Africans, including individuals who claim to be Muslims or Christians. The word "traditional" means indigenous, that which is aboriginal or foundational, handed down from generation to generation, upheld and practiced by Africans today. (p. 10)

Though it is an inheritance from generations ago, Awolalu emphasized that traditional African religion is treated not as a thing of the past but as that which connects the past with the present and the present with eternity. In this, the Sankofa bird, which moves forward by looking back, is symbolic (Tedli 1995). Thus do today's living men and women practice traditional religion. It is a religion that is based mainly on oral transmission and not written on paper but in peoples' hearts, minds, oral history, rituals, shrines, and religious functions. "It has no founders or reformers like Gautama the Buddha, Asoka, Christ, or Muhammad. It is not the religion of one hero. It has no missionaries, or even the desire to propagate the religion, or to proselytize" (Awolalu 1976, p. 10). A well-respected authority on African religion, John Mbiti (1990) described religion as the strongest element in the traditional background of an African and one that exerts probably the greatest influence upon the thinking and living of the people concerned.

Though Africa is a large continent with multitudes of nations, complex cultures, innumerable languages, and myriad dialects, traditional religion is still considered in the singular because there are many basic similarities in the religious systems. The religious practice is unified by the concept of God. God is considered the Supreme Being and is given different names by different people. Awolalu (1976) explained:

In Nigeria among the Yoruba people, He is called Olodumare. By meaning and connotation, this name signifies that the Supreme Being is unique, that His majesty is superlative, that He is unchanging and ever reliable. He is also called Olorun (the owner of Heaven), and Eleda (the Creator). The Edos call Him Osanobuwa, and this means God who is the "Source and Sustainer of the World". The Ibos call Him Chükwu, that is the Great Chi or the Great Source of life and of being. The Nupes call Him Soko, the Great One; He who dwells in Heaven; and they also designate him Tso-Ci meaning the Owner of us, the One to whom we belong. The Ewe-speaking people of Ghana speak of Him as Nana Buluku (Ancient of Days), and this suggests His eternity. (p. 15)

There is also the concept of divinities and/or spirits as well as beliefs in the ancestral cult. Every locality may and does have its own local deities, its own festivals, its own name, or names for the Supreme Being, but in essence the pattern is the same. There is that noticeable "Africanness" in the whole pattern. According to Oduyoye (1997), the African view of the world is nourished by a cosmology that is founded on a Source Being, the Supreme God, and other divine beings that are associated with God. As God is the foundation of life, nothing happens without God. God lives, God does not die, and so indeed humans do not die. Even when we do not occupy a touchable body, we still live on. She further wrote:

The immediacy of God in African affairs is also demonstrated through the God-related names we bear. Theophorous names like Nyamekye (gift of God) and Dardom (depend on God) are examples from Akan names. Yoruba names beginning with Olu or Oluwa speak of human experience of God. (p. 6)

In names, African ontology is centered on God who is the source of life and cohesion, whose sovereignty over all cannot be questioned. Writing about restitution and punishment, Mbiti (1990) claimed that the majority of African people believe that God punishes in this life. For that reason, misfortune may be interpreted as indicating that the sufferer has broken some moral or virtual contract with God.

The idea and structure of human society for traditional Africans, are essentially part of a worldview that is fundamentally holistic, sacred, and highly integrated. Human community, therefore, has its full meaning and significance within the transcendental center of ultimate meaning. Hence, the belief in ancestors and the supernatural order, in addition to its inherent religious import, provides traditional African groups a useful overarching system that helps people observe reality and impose divine authority and sanction to their life (Ejizu 1986, p. 20).

Kalu (2011) wrote, "The practical aspect of belief in African traditional religion is not only worship but also on...human conduct" (p. 26), explaining that belief in God and in the other spiritual beings implies a certain type of conduct, conduct that respects the order established by God and watched over by the divinities and the ancestors.

At the center of traditional African morality is human life. Africans are expected to have a sacred reverence for life, for it is believed to be the greatest of God's gifts to humans. To protect and nurture their lives, all human beings are inserted within a given community, and it is within this community that one works out one's destiny and every aspect of individual life. The dependency on community in African culture contradicts the highest level of Maslow's hierarchy: for it is not self-actualization but the sustenance of a collectivity that is highest. The promotion of life *within one's own community* is the determinant principle of African traditional morality, and this promotion is guaranteed only in the community. Living harmoniously within a community is a moral obligation ordained by God for the promotion of life. Religion provides the basic infrastructure on which this life-centered, community-oriented morality is based. John Mbiti's (1990) famous saying "I am because we are; and since we are, therefore I am," (p. 106) captures this ethical principle well. The implication is that one has an obligation to maintain harmonious relationships with all the members of the community and to do what is necessary to repair every breach of harmony and to strengthen the community bonds, especially through justice and sharing (Magessa 1997). This is not simply a social need but a religious obligation since God, the divinities and the ancestors, the guarantors of this order of things, are quick to punish defaulters. "Traditional African religion has no written legal documents showing what is legal or illegal, but traditional Africans have a code of conduct which they all know" (Adewale 1987, p. 8).

The colonial inheritance in Africa, described in Chap. 1 of this book, caused significant erosion of this cultural principle. The outcome of indirect rule was to increase the power of chiefs far more than tradition allowed, thus promoting abuse of power and tyranny. Self-enrichment replaced care of the community as the guiding force and traditional leadership became more like the aggrandizement of monarchs in Europe. In the words of Achebe (1959) in *Things Fall Apart*:

> The white man is very clever. He came quietly and peaceably with his religion. We were amused at his foolishness and allowed him to stay. Now he has won our brothers, and our clan can no longer act like one. He has put a knife on the things that held us together and we have fallen apart. (p. 30)

Boakye-Sarpong (1989) explained "In order to aid man in ethical living, God has put in him the 'oracle of the heart'... the 'inner oracle'... This 'oracle of the heart' is a person's conscience, the law of God written in him. A person is at peace when he obeys his conscience" (p. 6). When man disobeys this "inner oracle," he lives in constant fear, especially in fear of all natural manifestations of divine power. The Igbo express this in their proverb: *"Ọbụ onye ñụlụ iyi asị ka egbe igwe na-atụ egwu"*—It is only one who has committed perjury that is afraid of the thunder. Thunder is believed by many Africans to be a manifestation of divine power and is even sometimes regarded as a divinity. People often swear by this divinity, asking him to visit his wrath on them if what they say is not the truth.

Idowu (1973) wrote about the cosmic dimension of traditional African morality:

> Perhaps because of their strong attachment to the community, Africans have a very strong sense of justice. Without justice, life in the community would be impossible; there would be no harmony. A victim of injustice often makes a direct appeal to God. Africans believe that God, who is just and who sees and knows everything, hates injustice as is illustrated by the following Akan proverb: "*Nyame mpe kwaseabuo nti ena wama obiara edin*" (It is because God hates injustice that he has given each one a name). (p. 66)

Ejizu (n.d.) wrote that religion may be distinct and separate from morality, as many scholars have rightly argued, but in traditional Africa the line dividing the two is very thin. "African traditional religion plays a crucial role in the ethical dynamics of the different groups. In the traditional African background, 'gods serve as police men'" (p. 6). This concept was demonstrated in a Democracy Day Celebration in Nigeria when a retired Anglican Prelate, Bishop Peter Akinola, asked a congregation that included the country's president and his entourage to take corrupt officials "to the court of God." But the congregation failed to respond to this prayer. Apparently disappointed with this response, the clergyman replied angrily to the elite congregation:

See, it is very clear. You are not interested in fighting corruption. If you do, let us take our case to the court of God, if you dare. Who is deceiving who? You are only deceiving yourselves, not God. And you who is stealing government funds, subjecting the poor to untold hardship; you who steal oil subsidy money, making Nigerians pay for fuel through their noses; you who steal funds meant for improving our power supply, deliberately making Nigerians live a life in utter darkness, will you repent today? I doubt it! (Udo 2012, para. 5)

One does not need to be reminded that the preacher was addressing a congregation of government officials who have taken swearing oaths upon assumption of office but abandoned their moral and ethical foundation of their faith. Reverend Akinola further said:

This hydra headed monster (of corruption) has literally taken over the soul and eaten up the fabric of Nigeria. Officials steal our public funds openly by the pen, while others steal by the power of the gun. Successive governments have declared half-hearted war against corruption to no avail. We know only too well that the fight against corruption is largely selective directed at those opposing the government, with no strong political connection. Many of those fighting it (corruption) in police and Judiciary have no clean hands. When any National Assembly Committee or any government agency is inviting anybody for questioning it is because those being investigated have not yet given the agency inviting it their due share of the booty. (quoted in Udo 2012, para. 6–7)

According to Mbiti (1990) the belief behind oaths is that God, or some power higher than the individual man, will punish the person who breaks the requirements of the oath. Mbiti (1990) explained that in Africa, oaths are used as another method of establishing and maintaining good human relationships. Referring to the African philosophy of *Ubuntu*, Mbiti explained

Blood-brotherhood and blood-sisterhood oaths bind people mystically together. People, who are not immediately related, go through a ritual which often involves exchanging small amount of their blood by drinking or rubbing it into each other's body. Such oath places great moral and mystical obligations upon the parties concerned. Such oaths are taken when people join secret societies or bound to do evil deeds. (p. 56)

While Mbiti's human philosophy has to do with collective personhood, interconnectedness, and collective morality and solidarity, it indicates an apparent natural synergy between *Ubuntu* and Christian values inherent in oath taking. Louw (1998) suggested that *Ubuntu* has a spiritual dimension that should not be underestimated and has been the source of inspiration to theologians and clergy alike.

The influence of oath taking on the life of an African in general, and Nigerians in particular, might even be linked to some of the oath takers at the Association of Nigerians Against Corruption (ANAC) seminars in Nigeria and the USA. Participants might have been motivated by their faith, upbringing, or other forces, as we will see. The need to allow the participant to talk about their life revealed clues to their considerations in taking a voluntary oath.

Earlier, I traced the origin of corruption in Nigeria and also described the upsurge of corruption in recent decades. It seems that the menace of corruption has defied all treatments, and the damage done to national life cannot be quantified. The toga of corruption is still shining brightly like a menacing star in the sky with its visible symptoms: poor economic policy, underdevelopment of civil society, and the weak accountability of public institutions. All these translate to what every Nigerian experiences each day:

1. Lack of electricity;
2. Bad roads;
3. Queues at gas stations;
4. Police extortion on the highways;
5. Immigration and customs extortion;
6. Slow movement of files through offices;
7. Port congestion; and
8. Election irregularities.

This study draws from the above concepts of Maslow (1943) and Thalhammer et al. (2007). Maslow's list of fundamental needs (Fig. 2.1) can be useful for understanding motivation to act for change of Nigerian society, described in Chap. 1, as one with a breakdown of law and order where immorality, poverty, lack of security, lack of employment, and lack of respect for others reign.

This study finds support in Thalhammer et al.'s (2007) theory of "Factors Affecting the Process of Responding to Injustice," which relate to Maslow's theory. The acts of injustice in this book relate to bribery and corruption with all its ramifications, which lead to immorality, poverty, lack of security, lack of employment, and lack of respect for law and order. Thalhammer et al. theorize and enumerate what can make someone become a resister against these injustices; the study applies this to Nigeria and the role of ANAC.

CHAPTER 3

My Interviews with the Oath Takers

Abstract The chapter begins by connecting the oath-taking initiative to the author's life experience. The nature and strengths of the method of choice—narrative inquiry through interviews—is considered, followed by an account of the seminars of the Association of Nigerians Against Corruption (ANAC). Methods for gathering data through interviews are then described including selecting the sample of 15 participants, the approach and rationale of interviews by telephone, the main questions asked, and the handling of data (transcription, triangulation, and coding).

Keywords Study · Biographical research · ANAC seminars · Population · Data sampling · Data analysis

THE STORY OF MY LIFE IN THIS STUDY

The purpose of this study is to find out why people take a voluntary public oath to shun corruption with all its ramifications and apply these findings to other anti-corruption campaigns of ANAC. What happened in their lives to make them come to that decision? How does taking the oath impact their lives? What motivates them to take the oath? What roles does their religion play in their actions? These are the questions I tried to answer.

Positionality

In narrative research the researcher should indicate their own relationship to the study and its subject matter: This begins with basics: "their presence in the research and the influence of social background, for example gender, race, social class, or religion" (Roberts 2011, p. 13). Roberts concluded that placing the researcher fully within the research is "to recognize that we all have stories and it seems a fundamental part of social interaction to tell our tales" (p. 14). I told my story to all the participants in the study.

My story in relation to corruption and its prevention began in 1957, when I joined an anti-corruption vanguard Nigerian League of Bribes Corner. My family upbringing, my religious background, and an oath taking have seen me through a morally guided life till today. My own experience motivated me to do the research and write this book. My story is not new to the participants as it was told at every seminar that the participants in this study have attended. They are aware, through my story, of how my moral upbringing has helped to guide my behavior in the face of temptations to be corrupt. This has implications for the way the participants might have perceived me or responded to me.

WHY NARRATIVE INQUIRY?

According to Kenny (2006), narrative inquiry invites the reader into a story. It helps to elaborate complexities and relationships in understanding human life. "Narrative studies are flourishing as a means of understanding the personal identity, lifestyle, culture, and historical world of the narrator" (Lieblich et al. 1998, p. 20). Kvale and Brinkmann (2009) suggested that if you want to know how people understand their world and their lives, talk to them, or rather encourage them to talk and listen to what they have to say about their lives. Through conversation, we get to know other people and learn their experiences, feeling, attitudes, and the world they live in. Having convinced that upbringing, religion, and oath shaped my life, I became interested in the biographical stories of others.

The biographical research method became popular in the early decades of the twentieth century before the rise of quantitative methods of research. Telling life stories—and stories more general—seemed to be in decline by the early part of the twentieth century. In 1936, the literary theorist and critic Walter Benjamin sadly concluded that with the rise of impersonal media and urban culture, the storyteller has already become something remote from us and the art of storytelling is coming to an end. Yet a resurgence had already begun, first in sociology and then spreading throughout qualitative social inquiry. This can be traced to the Chicago School of Sociology. According to Apitzsch and Siouti (2007), two sociologists, William Isaac Thomas and Florian Znaniecki of Chicago, were the pioneers of biographical research in the discipline of sociology.

Biographical methods have claimed an increasing place in academic research and are alive and well in various academic disciplines. Roberts (2011) noted that a key debate within much of biographical research weighs the merits of "realism" versus "constructionism" in the study of lives. He explained that realism holds that there is some objective knowledge of reality that stories reflect. He also explained that for constructionists, at the extreme, the view that life stories reflect reality or empirical truth is simplistic and misconceived, what Bourdieu (1986) had called the "biographical illusion." Miller and Brewer (2003) stated that biographical researchers should take a pragmatic stance in research instead of a firm allegiance to "realism" or "constructionism." A pragmatic approach will lay emphasis on purpose and gain insights into individual lives rather than dwelling on differences in methodological and theoretical assumption.

The structures of life story in biographical method provide meanings and thereby define the people and circumstances within the research process. My research is about very delicate matters, which cannot be molded into surveys or structured interviews, but demand great sensitivity on my part as the researcher. It requires an environment in which the participants can trust the researcher. According to Miller and Brewer (2003), "biographical method in research is the collection and analysis of an intensive account of a whole life or portion of a life, usually by an in-depth, unstructured interview" (p. 6). The placement of an individual within a nexus of social connections, historical events, and life experiences is considered vital. Bloor and Wood (2006) wrote that the biographical method involves the detailed reconstruction of individual life stories. They asserted that biographies enable the understanding of individual lives set within their social contexts by tracing the circumstances, choices, constraints, and decisions that affect people's lives. This is important for my study because data for the study come from the live history of the participants as they tell the story of their lives.

It is generally accepted, then, that the purpose of a biographical study is to gain insights into the everyday experiences of individual lives.

Roberts (2011) remarked that in life stories commonly referred to as "real events and experiences," the tellers may be the only witness to such happenings. The study is a gathering of testimonies from participants about their perceptions, attitudes to, and experiences of (attempted) corruption. Hence, a study on what motivates individuals to take a public oath against corruption at a seminar can find this method suitable to search the life story of the individuals who took the oath.

My study upon which this book is based is on constructivist, interpretative, and phenomenological paradigms. These paradigms assume that reality is co-created, that meaning in human action is inherent in that action, and that knowledge about things can only be described as one experience it (Schwandt 2001). Guba and Lincoln (2005) wrote that a significant portion of social phenomena consist of the meaning-making activities of groups and individuals around some phenomena. They described the meaning-making activities as the central interest to social constructionist/constructivist activities that shape action or inaction. My questions revolve around how meaning is made and shaped by the participants of the study as they tell their stories.

According to Charmaz (2006), an interpretative view of theory development emphasizes that the very understanding gained from the theory rests on the theorist's interpretation of the studied phenomenon and aims to show patterns and connections rather than causality. The themes that emerged from this study were based on interpretive frames used to code the participants' view that shaped their reality, as well as my own. From a phenomenological point of view, it is apparent that the focus of my study is on how activities in the lives of the participants from youth to adolescence made a meaningful transition into their decision to take an oath against corruption.

The role of a biographical researcher has been of concern to many writers. Sparkes (1994) and Atkinson (1998) have raised questions within the corpus of the literature on this subject regarding subjective interpretations and judgments of the researchers. They questioned how much the researcher should reveal in sharing stories not to impinge on building trust and establishing credibility. In my case, I explained to the participants of every seminar how my upbringing socially and religiously made me who I am today. I supported my statements with credible letters of commendations and various awards I have received. The disclosure of my achievements and show of credible documents in support of my claim of consistent resistance against corruption may have created trust and integrity. My example may have encouraged them to live up to the oath as well.

On the other hand, if they failed to keep the oath, it could be more difficult for them to confess in interviews that they did not live up to the oath as well as I had.

The main idea of the biographical-narrative interview as used in the study was to generate a spontaneous autobiographical narration, not significantly structured by questions posed by the interviewer but by the narrator's structures of relevance. Josselson and Lieblich (1995) asserted that narrative approaches to understanding bring the researcher more closely into the investigative process than do quantitative and statistical methods. They argued that through narrative, we come in contact with our participants as people engaged in the process of interpreting themselves. "We decode, recognize, re-contextualize, or abstract their life in the interest of reaching a new interpretation of the raw data of experience before us" (p. ix).

About the ANAC Seminars

Let me give some background information about the seminars and its participants at the time. Between June 1984 and November 2011, I conducted seven seminars on corruption under the banner of Association of Nigerians against Corruption (ANAC). At the end of each seminar many participants voluntarily took a public oath not to give or receive a bribe and not to participate in any corrupt practices for the rest of their lives.

The first ANAC seminar on corruption in which people came forward to take a public oath was held at Ahmadu Bello University, Zaria, in June 1984. The presence of Nigerian dignitaries gave legitimacy to the vanguard. The occasion, which was chaired by the traditional ruler of Zaria, Emir Alhaji Shehu Idris, was attended by the Vice Chancellor of the university, Professor Ango Abdullahi, Deputy Commander of the Nigerian Army School in Zaria, Lieutenant Colonel Tunde Akogun, who swore in the 40 participants who took the oath, the priest of the church on campus, as well as the imam of the mosque on campus. Nigeria was then under the military government of Major General Muhammadu Buhari, which had launched a campaign labeled the "War against Indiscipline."

In 1987, yet another military coup brought in a new government. Individuals that I had never met approached me and advised me to stop the activities of ANAC at Ahmadu Bello University where I was teaching. My refusal may have led to the series of burglaries that followed in my residence along with the theft of my car by some unknown people who promised to give it back to me upon payment of a bribe. These experiences of burglaries, theft, and fear of the unknown led me to return to the USA with my family in 1988.

In 2000, democracy returned to Nigeria, and elected president Olusegun Obasanjo vowed to fight corruption. I had the privilege of being invited back to Nigeria early in his regime. In July 2001, ANAC was re-launched as a non-governmental organization in the nation's capital, Abuja. The occasion was graced by the presence of the Honorable Kanu Agabi, Minister of Solid Mineral Development, representing President Obasanjo, and by the Supreme Court Justice, Katsina Alu, who swore in some of the oath takers. The occasion was chaired by the Chairman of Independent Corrupt Practice Commission, Justice Mustapha Akanbi. Twenty-five youths and adults took the oath against corruption. This was followed a week later by another seminar at the University of Ibadan where 20 more people took the same oath.

A fourth seminar took place in April 2008 at the Leadership Institute in the central Nigerian city of Jos, with 13 students' executive members from Abubakar Tafawa Balewa University, University of Abuja, and University of Jos participating. All 13 students and 9 non-student participants took the oath against corruption. In another seminar organized by Oyo State Ministry of Education, held in Ibadan in June 2010, eight graduate students of the University of Ibadan joined the vanguard by taking the anti-corruption oath.

A seminar designed to bring a change of attitude and perception among Nigerians in the Diaspora in order to reduce corruption in Nigeria was held in Dayton, Ohio, in June 2011. Fifty Nigerians residing in Dayton attended while the Nigerian Ambassador to Canada led 20 of the participants in taking the anti-corruption oath. The latest seminars took place in November 2011 and 2013 at Efon-Alaaye's Nigerian Youth Service Corps camp. Twenty-eight of the participants took the public oath against corruption in 2011 and 20 in 2013. Each of the seminars included high-profile people and other dignitaries providing an extra dimension of solemnity to the event and to the meaning of taking the oath.

The population for this study came from the Abuja, Ibadan, Efon-Alaaye, Jos, Zaria, and Dayton seminars. Many of the oath takers in Abuja, Ibadan, Efon-Alaaye, and Jos continue to reside in Nigeria where they are still faced with the problems of corruption; the 20 oath takers in Dayton are living in the USA, where they are probably less confronted with day-to-day incidents of business, political, and public service corruption. The common denominator among the Nigerian and Dayton participants is that they were all born in Nigeria, grew up in Nigeria, and must have gone through similar conditions of life in Nigeria. At the same time, this two-country research, I thought, might also reveal to what extent corruption in their lives depends on being in Nigeria. Travel back to Nigeria was a requirement for selection as research participants, because I assumed that they would be more prone to everyday corruption there than in the US.

In the seminars, participants were exposed to topics related to the danger of corruption to individual, family, and nation. Invited speakers talked about their life experiences and how they have been able to suppress the temptation of benefiting from a corrupt life. Each person that took an oath against corruption received a membership card as a reminder of the oath, which they could display to would-be perpetrators if confronted by a situation where a bribe or any other corrupt practice arose.

At the time of this study, only 12 out of the 20 who swore an oath at the Dayton seminar still live in the area. Twenty-two participants took the oath in Jos and are employed in different parts of northern Nigeria. For the purpose of the interviews for this study, I was able to locate six of them living in three different states of Nigeria. I also found two more of the participants from the Ibadan and Efon-Alaaye seminars, making a total of 17 participants. Three additional participants from the Zaria and Abuja seminars were located, bringing the sample population to 20.

By quantitative research standards the sample is small, but the worth of the results of this study rest on the life stories of individuals and not on the number represented by the total oath takers. I have not tried to prove hypotheses but to call wider attention to factors that lead to courageous commitments, so badly needed in Nigeria and other African nations. This research employed a qualitative case study research design using telephone interviews. The pros and cons of using telephone interviews are discussed in the section below on the data collection method.

DATA GATHERING AND ANALYSIS

Merrill and West (2009) referenced three sampling methods:

- Opportunistic sampling;
- Criterion sampling;
- Snowball sampling;

Opportunistic sampling takes place when the researcher takes advantage of a situation to interview individuals, through luck, chance, the right word being said, or because people offer themselves (Miles and Huberman 1994). The participants for this study had attended similar seminars with the same objectives at different times and locations, so they were not opportunistic participants. Yet, at the same time, there was an opportunistic element in the sense that I was willing to take whoever I could trace from the list.

According to Creswell (1998), criterion sampling occurs when all individuals studied represent people who have experienced the same phenomenon. The individuals in this study went through similar seminars given by ANAC. The objectives of the seminars were the same, and the participants had equal opportunity to take the same anti-corruption oath. This study will fit into the category of criterion sampling.

Snowball sampling is used when participants are selected through reference either by other participants or by contacts of the researcher. This strategy was not relevant for this study as I had a complete list of names from the seminar lists. This being said, I want to mention that participants did help me locate two of the Jos seminar participants through their fellow participants at the seminar. The majority of participants were found through phone number and e-mail address record keeping.

Knox and Burkard (2009) reminded us that another decision that qualitative interviewers face involves the actual means of completing the interview. Hiller and DiLuzio (2004) claimed that the face-to-face interview allows the observation not only of verbal but also nonverbal data. Carr and Worth (2001) observed that when participant and interviewer are in the same room they have access to facial expressions, gestures, and other para-verbal communications that may enrich the meaning of the spoken words. This opportunity may enable the participants and interviewer to build the rapport that may enable the participants to freely disclose their experiences more effectively than might occur in phone interviews. Polkinghorne (1994) stated that in-person interviews yield authentic and deep descriptions of phenomena via the interviewer's ability to facilitate trust and openness with the interviewee. This will then lessen the interviewee's need for impression management and enable the examination of his or her private experience. This is about interaction between researcher and participant.

Shuy (2003) indicated that little research has compared the benefits of these means of data collection.

Knox and Burkard (2009) confirmed that phone interviews are quite common because they enable researchers to include participants from virtually any geographic region, as no one is required to travel. Musselwhite et al. (2006) echoed other studies by writing that phone interviews are more economical, minimize disadvantages of in-person interviews, and improve the quality of data collection. A phone interview also eliminates the challenges of traveling for both researcher and participants. Each party may conduct the interview in the comfort of their homes instead of one or both traveling to a specific location.

I chose to do telephone interviews rather than face-to-face interviews in the study for two important reasons: my personal relationship to the participants and certain uncontrollable situations in Nigeria at the time of the study. My relation to the participants as the founder of ANAC, the NGO that forms the basis for their taking of the oath being studied, could be considered an asset, but it could also pose an ethical problem as a researcher. I know all the participants, and they all know me. About six of the participants are close associates of mine. Everyone was excited when I called to inform them of the study. I wondered if they would see me as an "expert" who initiated them into the context of ANAC where they decided to take the oath. If so, how free would they be in the encounter to talk about any failures or other shortcomings they had had in keeping their oath—or, alternatively, to be critical of the whole approach? Interview situations have a very asymmetric power (Karnieli-Miller et al. 2009). My physical presence could be a hindrance to the participants telling the truth. Additionally, African culture promotes respect for elders. As I am older than the majority of the participants, the younger participants might not be as comfortable with me face to face as they would be in a telephone interview. How to avoid these risks became a matter of deep concern for me. While it could not be totally avoided, avoiding face-to face interviewing reduced the ethical problem of subtle intimidation of the interviewees. A phone interview could reduce the effects of such a situation as the absence of eye-to-eye contact might arouse less fear in the participants and they might be more forthcoming if they believe that they would never cross paths with me soon or at all after completing the research.

I take satisfaction in the free-willing responses I got from all the participants, as there were no hesitations or gaps for rethinking in their stories.

A second more exceptional and negative factor came into my selection of telephone interviewing. The insurgency of terrorists known as Boko Haram was prominent in the northern part of Nigeria during the study period.

This militant Islamic sect is violently against Western education in Northern Nigeria, and its followers have attacked and killed people in Abuja, Jos, Maiduguri, and other cities in the region. Abuja, Jos, and Zaria were venues of some of the seminars conducted in this study. Many of the participants in Nigeria are still residing in Abuja, Jos, and other northern cities. It was unsafe to travel around in the area, especially as I was conducting a study about educating people on how to combat corruption from the grassroots level. A telephone interview rather than a face-to-face interview eliminated the risk of encountering the terrorists for both the researcher and participants. People were even afraid to spend much time on the phone because of the rumor that Boko Haram has the capability of making cell phones explode as a means of attacking their victims. Getting participants to stay on the phone long was a difficult task, which might have impacted the duration and depth of the conversations. At the beginning of each interview, I encouraged the participants to talk freely about their lives before and after taking the oath at the seminar. I gave similar trigger questions to each participant after their consent approval to do the interview. These trigger questions focused on the purpose of the study, thus enabling all the participants to talk about the same topics sharing different experiences.

- Why did you take a voluntary public oath against corruption?
- What has happened in your life to make you take that decision?
- Has the ANAC seminar played a role in that decision and how?
- Does the oath have an impact on your life and how?
- Are there temptations, when, where, and how often?
- Has the oath impacted your relation with family, friends, and work mates?
- Have you kept the oath all the time? What made it possible?
- If not, what made it difficult for you to keep the oath all the time?
- Do you talk to other people about the oath?
- Has the oath had an impact on your children and other children you contact?

I did not stick rigidly to any order, but instead let each participant took the interview in the direction where he or she felt their experience was most worth talking about; I had my questions at hand and could still ensure that all topics were eventually covered but in a flow comfortable to each. Insights from the answers to the above questions were used to fine-tune the interview as was necessary.

The Selection and Interviewing of Participants for the Study

As the ANAC Chair, I had access to a partial list of oath takers during the 1983–2013 period, which I used as a point of departure for selecting participants. There are about 1000 oath takers on the list, of whom 600 were linked to their telephone or e-mail addresses. Not every oath taker chose to give information about themselves during the seminars. The identified participants fall into four groups as follows:

- Jos group: 12 people
- Dayton group: 20 people
- Efon-Alaaye group: 18 people
- Other groups (Zaria, Abuja, Ibadan): 10 people

The list of the 600 people I identified by their phone or e-mail addresses was the starting point. Only 60 was current. As it happened, the list was made up of almost equal number of men and women, with ages ranging between 21 and 70. In order to achieve a variety in terms of gender and age representation, the female and male participants were listed separately, each group in the age orders. I then proceeded with a random selection, marking every third name on each of the two lists to compose a list of 20 participants. I chose 20 as a maximum number because I expected that I would have reached saturation by then. This sampling method guaranteed participants from both genders, a variety of age groups, and the five sites of the seminar. The entire group of the 20 selected participants initially responded positively to the consent form; however, only 15 of them made themselves available for the interview. After receiving the consent forms, I scheduled all the interviews to take place within the same time period. I waited for the five people who failed to answer or return my calls. I have very close relationships with two of the five who did not make themselves available for the interview. It then dawned on me that over the years since they took the oath these two friends of mine may have experienced embarrassing situations at work or with other associates. I assume that due to such embarrassing calamities they might have withdrawn even after signing the consent form. I made efforts to contact more females so that I could achieve more gender balance in the numbers. After several phone calls that did not yield any results, I settled for 15 out of 20 in order not to lose those who had already agreed to set up an interview time. The interviews were

Table 3.1 Profile of participants interviewed

Participants by Interview Order	Gender	Age Category	Location of Seminar (Year Attended)	Location of Present Abode
1	Male	41–45	Jos (2008)	Markurdi
2	Female	51+	Abuja (2001)	Abuja
3	Male	18–25	Efon-Alaaye (2011)	Akure
4	Female	36–40	Jos (2008)	Ado-Ekiti
5	Male	51+	Dayton (2011)	Dayton, OH
6	Female	51+	Zaria (1984)	Newark, NJ
7	Female	31–35	Dayton (2011)	Dayton, OH
8	Female	41–45	Abuja (2001)	London, UK
9	Male	41–45	Jos (2008)	Abuja
10	Male	46–50	Jos (2008)	Ado-Ekiti
11	Female	36–40	Jos (2008)	Abuja
12	Male	46–50	Dayton (2011)	Dayton, OH
13	Male	36–40	Efon-Alaaye (2011)	Port Harcourt
14	Male	51+	Dayton (2011)	Dayton, OH
15	Male	51+	Ibadan (2001)	Ibadan

held between December 2013 and April 2014. Table 3.1 summarizes information on the participants in terms of gender, age, where they took the ANAC seminar, and where they lived at the time of the interview.

In total, nine males and six females were interviewed. The age range was from young adults (age group 18–25) to middle age and older (51 plus). The seminar locations of the participants were as follows:

- Abuja (two participants)
- Dayton (four participants)
- Efon (two participants)
- Jos (five participants)
- Ibadan (one participant)
- Zaria (one participant)

Each interview lasted between 45 min and 1 hr. It should be noted that the participants dwelling in Nigeria live with corruption every day of their lives and have more intense day-to-day experience with corruption than those living in the US.

I transcribed each interview the same day I conducted it. "Transcribing interviews from oral to a written mode, structures the interview conversations in a form amenable to closer analysis, and is in itself an initial analytic process" (Kvale and Brinkmann 2009, p. 103). The same authors also suggested that there is no basic rule in transcribing except to say in the report how the transcriptions were made. Merrill and West (2009) reported that they normally transcribe their interviews in full in their narrative form. They made no attempt to force speech into a written or grammatical correctness. They indicated pauses with three dots, and where material is abbreviated or omitted in the process of editing or quotation, they use four dots. Merrill and West transcribed their interview in a manner consistent with the rhythms and patterns of speech. Kvale and Brinkmann did not raise objection to this approach of transcribing. They indicated that since there is no universal form of code for transcribing research interviews, the choice will depend on the intended use of the transcript, whether for a detailed linguistic or conversational analysis or for reporting the subject's accounts in a readable public way.

The transcription of the interviews was done verbatim from the oral versions. I transcribed the interview for readability without forcing the report to grammatical correctness. The objective was to understand, noting the level of emotional expression attached to each story as it may have bearing on the meaning of the interview. I read the transcript over three times. As I read each transcript I envisioned the image of the participant before me without looking for the name. The response became part of me as I identified similar experiences among the participants.

"One of the most common techniques used to enhance credibility of instrumentation is triangulation" (McMillan and Wergin 2010, p. 91). Triangulation refers to a method used for checking and establishing the validity of the methodology used. In using narrative and biographical methods, questions of validity have a different meaning than in quantitative research. The triangulation used in the study is called the *member check* (Lincoln and Guba 1985, p. 314). Thereby, I shared the transcription of the interview with the participants—the source—so they could have an opportunity to check and review the data materials and provide further responses to the research questions. This helped to verify and validate information that I transcribed from the recorded interview. Transcripts were e-mailed to participants to check the accuracy of what I reported. Not everyone responded speedily. The reply spread over a 2-week period as I followed up with phone calls. Thirteen of the 15 participants responded that the transcript was correct as reported. One of the remaining two wrote, "That's okay except for some grammatical corrections here and there that I would have loved to correct if my name is going to be on the line!!! People expect some level of English mastery from some of us." I responded to the participant not to worry about the English and that the way we speak is different from the way we write. I informed him that I transcribed the interview verbatim and that I am the only one who reads the transcript with the name of the participant on it. I assured him that everything would be destroyed after the study was over as stated in the consent letter and that no name would be published in the final dissertation. The last person to respond warned me about the sensitive information she has given me and wanted reassurance that it would not be published with her name. Again I assured her that what was said in the consent letter will be strictly followed.

Data Analysis

Analyzing data involves "thinking that is self-conscious, systematic, organized, and instrumental" (Schatzman and Strauss 1973, p. 109). It is an interactive process between the researcher and his or her experience and data. It helps the researcher to discover significant classes of things, persons, events, and properties that characterize them. I did a thematic analysis to identify possible patterns and also relevant experiences that might not be shared by others. The thematic process used in this study was adapted from Barbara Merrill's analytical stages (Merrill and West 2009).

- I read the transcript again and again and made thematic comments in the margin, such as the impact of family, school, religion, seminar, peers, college, society, resistance, commitment, and so on. The more I read the transcript, the more I got to know the person.
- I wrote a summary about each person and identified themes such as initial schooling experiences, the impact of the family on morality, and the impact of religion. I included relevant quotes from the interview in the summary as such summaries reminded me of each participant.
- For reasons of anonymity, I only identified the participants by initials.
- I identified common themes and issues and categorized across the stories.
- I related the data to theory and to the research questions drawing on existing knowledge.
- The answering of the research questions with the help of the data produced the results of the study.

Coding is a process by which data are broken down, conceptualized, and put back together in new ways (Strauss and Corbin 1990). It involves identifying concepts and themes from the interviews and notes in the overall comparison of the transcript. Writing about coding, Eriksson and Kovalainen (2008) noted that in case study research preplanned systematic coding is most often used. The emphasis is on the production of detailed and holistic knowledge based on the analysis of multiple empirical sources rich in context. They further explained that biographical studies, such as used here, draw on the qualitative research tradition emphasizing interpretation and understanding of the cases as well as elaborating of cultural meaning and sense making process of specific contexts. The main aim is to understand and explore the case from the inside and develop understanding from the perspective of the people involved in the case.

As I read individual transcripts, I looked for shared experiences and patterns that connect across the transcripts. Observation on ethical and moral justification is an important factor in this study. I looked for the understanding of moral standards, logical and moral reasoning, and consistency in moral actions in the life story of the participants. Many of the participants gave credit to their upbringing and religion. They had pride in their inner satisfaction for keeping their oath. These individual stories became a collective story.

Lieblich et al. (1998) noted that data collected as a story can be the object of the research or a means for the study of another question. It may be used for comparison among groups, to learn about a social phenomenon or historical period, or to explore a personality. The study for this book is only to explore the experience of the individual in respect to the issue of corruption in Nigeria in view of having taken an oath against corruption.

Kvale (1996) recommended that after the participants have described their lived world, the following three adapted steps are useful:

- Note new relationships and new meanings that are revealed.
- Condense and interpret the meaning of what participants describe.
- Transcribe and interpret interview either alone or with other researchers.

I used the above approaches to condense, categorize, structure narration, and interpret. Observations, sentences, and paragraphs were coded, and each element was given a name or coding. Every coded item was then placed into a series of categories that resulted in motivating factors, impact of the oath, and episodes. Three helpful stages arose from the approach:

- Noticing relevant phenomena;
- Collecting examples of those phenomena;
- Analyzing those phenomena in order to find commonalities, differences, patterns, and structures.

Lieblich et al. (1998) labeled these criteria for evaluating narrative inquiry as providing:

- Width: the comprehensiveness of evidence;
- Coherence: the way different parts of the interpretation create a complete and meaningful picture;
- Insightfulness: the sense of innovation or originality in the presentation of the story and its analysis;
- Parsimony: the ability to provide an analysis based on a small number of concepts and elegance or aesthetic appeal (pp. 2–3).

This chapter has established how I am closely related to this study. I have experienced every listed purpose of the study. As the researcher, my story is told to the participants during the seminars they attended. My upbringing, religion, and oath taking shaped my life.

I used biographical research methods in the study to reduce the effect of being biased in asking the participants questions relating to my experience instead of those relating to their experience. Follow-up questions during the interview were based on the information from the narrative of the participants.

The study of this book is based on constructivist, interpretative, and phenomenological paradigms focusing on how activities in the lives of the participants from youth to adolescence provided meaning in their lives. Details of such activities were collected through telephone interview. A live face-to-face interview might have given me more meaning by interpreting the body language of the participants, but, as discussed, could have negatively affected the candor with which participants responded.

CHAPTER 4

Research Findings: Motives and Impacts of Oath Taking

Abstract This chapter reveals the narrative of the interview and classifies the results into 11 motive categories. It explains how the qualitative study on a thematic concept revealed that the motivating factors and impact of the oath have an influence on the participants in keeping their oath. The chapter closes with a table showing what the storytelling in the interviews indicated about participants' life experiences, upbringing, religion, seminar, peers and the impact.

Keywords Research findings · Motivating factors · Impact of oath taking · Episodes

> I am aware of the problems of corruption in Nigeria before the ANAC seminar. As a result of corruption, crime has gone up in the country because the law enforcement agencies have been found to be in collusion with people of the underground. I have always been pondering on what to do and how change can be effected. The seminar encouraged me and gave me an opportunity. Hence I took the oath.
> — (An oath-taker/participant from Abuja during interview)

This chapter draws on the first-hand stories about the events in the lives of the participants before and after taking the anti-corruption oath. Having employed Merrill and West's (2009) thematic steps, I used Eriksson and

Kovalainen's (2008) thematic analysis to identify themes emerging from the transcripts. Eriksson and Kovalainen concede that many of our temperament traits are evident at birth, but other characteristics such as trust, guilt, and competency are learned based upon our life experiences and the support we receive as we grow and develop. Hence, I inferred three main themes from the stories of the participants. These reflect the questions about motivating factors, the impact of the oath, and episodes from the story.

Motivating Factors

Corruption Awareness

The main purpose of my study was to find out what motivated the participants to take the voluntary oath against corruption during the ANAC seminar they attended and how this gives meaning to the oath in their lives. Each participant had more than one reason for taking the oath. All 15 participants acknowledged that they were aware of the high degree of corruption that exists in Nigeria; hence, they wanted to do something about it. The Abuja female participant whose words began this chapter traced her decision to take the oath to the rampant corruption she felt all around her and throughout Nigerian society. She indicated that the seminar had helped her to see the connection between the broad political and the everyday personal dimensions of this ubiquitous dishonesty.

Another female participant in the Abuja seminar currently living in the United States put it this way, "I am aware of the negative impact of corruption both in Nigeria and here in the US." She claimed that before she joined ANAC, she had had her own share of being a victim of corruption while she was living in Nigeria. She talked about corruption that exists among politicians, civil servants, and even in the market where exploitation of customers takes place regularly. "I bribed officials to get my children into elite secondary schools. I bribed to get a government job and witnessed how politicians heading the government ministries manipulated the budget to their interest. The police, immigration, customs are robbers in uniform." In Chapter II, I reviewed Ksenia's (2008) categorization of such practices as bureaucratic, political, and grand corruption.

Another female participant in the Abuja seminar claimed to have attended the seminar to see what she could contribute to make a difference. She said:

> I took the oath because I was concerned at the rate which corruption has eaten to the fabrics of Nigeria. Younger people like us should fight corruption. I am even afraid to finish college because there is no job. Many graduates are roaming the street and getting into crime to make ends meet. The oath will ginger me up to fight corruption in all its ramifications.

A male participant who took the oath in Dayton said to me in the interview:

> I joined ANAC and took the oath because I realized that there are some Nigerians who are likeminded and believe that our society have lost a number of opportunities through brain drain, as a result of corruption, hence we should do something.

He lamented about how the Nigerian politicians have drained the wealth of the nation by stashing money abroad instead of using it for development at home.

A male participant in the Efon-Alaaye seminar put the blame of corruption on everyone when he said:

> There is corruption everywhere and we are all guilty of it. We are the givers and the receivers. For example sexual corruption and bribery is common on our university campuses. But it takes two to tango. That's why I took the oath. Curbing corruption in Nigeria should start from the individual and not blaming our leaders for everything.

In sum, and not surprisingly, then, the awareness of just how pervasive and negative in effect corruption has become in Nigeria from the highest political to the everyday street level was on the minds of those who took the oath through ANAC.

To Be Part of a Vanguard

A second motivating factor that emerged in the stories of those participants I interviewed was a desire to be part of something positive and new.

Three of the participants stated in their story that they attended the seminar with the mindset of joining the anti-corruption vanguard. A male participant in the Ibadan seminar put it this way:

> I remember one American president said that "people who refused to participate in an action that can bring change will all the time be ruled and controlled by people who are not as clever as they are." Once I remember that statement, it becomes imperative for me or any right thinking Nigerian to join ANAC by taking the oath against corruption. This is what prompted me to take the oath.

A male participant in the Jos seminar said, "I chose to take the oath because I wanted to be part of a group campaigning against corruption. What I know about ANAC encouraged me." A male participant in the Dayton seminar also had his mind set to be a vanguard member: "taking the oath to me is a means of setting a boundary publicly. I always believe an individual should stand for something or else will fall for anything."

Upbringing

Thirteen of the participants credited their parents for their virtuous upbringing. They talked about the morality and the religious ethics under which they were raised. In some cases one could not separate the moral upbringing from the religious upbringing as a male participant in the Jos seminar said. "My father was a strict religious man. He raised us by the Quran. I will raise my children to be honest in whatever they do." Another participant, a female from the Abuja seminar, stated: "I come from a religious family and we have always been told to do what is right, speak the truth no matter what the consequences." Yet another participant, a male from the Jos seminar, credited his father. "In my family my father talked all the time about the danger of corruption. He encouraged us to be honest. My father's orientation made me took the oath."

Talking about his upbringing by his father, another male participant in the Jos seminar said:

> My late father raised all his children that we should not tell lies because it cannot benefit us. I tried to live on such instruction while in primary, secondary and the university by telling fifty percent of truth. Among all the children, I was the only one that tells that much of truth and my father noticed it.

A female participant in the Efon-Alaaye seminar, acknowledging her parents stated, "My parents have always demonstrated to us to be good and do the right thing. My parents were very strict the way we were brought up. We were trained not to lie, or be deceitful."

Another homage to the father from a male participant in the Jos seminar was like this:

> One of the people that I respect greatly is my father. He was a retired Warrant Officer Class II in the Nigerian Army. My father was an honest man. He had the opportunity to enrich himself while in the military, but he did not. He always tells us that what does not belong to you is not yours.

Similarly, telling about how he was raised, one male Dayton seminar participant put it this way:

> I was raised with very strict values with regards to expectations for myself and others. These strict values consider corruption or any illegal practices to be absolutely unacceptable and un-defendable. I have thus fostered that in every aspect of my life from my younger days till now.

It is not surprising that it was only fathers that got the accolades from both male and female participants. Nigeria is a patriarchal society in which the father as the head of family gives directions and instructions on how to raise the children. I could relate to the admiration of the father in this regard because my father was the family disciplinarian and the one that talked about how to live our lives honestly while my mother always unquestioningly dotted the i's and crossed the t's as she was asked to do.

Religion

Religion has played a significant role in the lives of the participants that acknowledged it. Five participants gave credit to their religion as either Muslims or Christians. "My father was a Muslim," an Abuja female participant said. "He raised me strictly in Islamic way. But later in life I became a Christian and accepted Jesus into my life. That has made it more possible for me to keep my oath." Another participant, a female of the Dayton seminar, said, "I took the oath because of my religious belief. As a Christian we have been told that corruption is a crime against humanity, against God." Yet another participant, a female from the Abuja seminar, gave thanks to God by saying, "I give thanks to God for the Christian way in which I was brought up. I raised my children the same way. Never to compromise, but do the right thing, the right way." A religious responsibility also encouraged her to keep her oath when she said:

> Being a leader in the church also helped me to be strong in keeping my oath. I know I have to be a good example. My belief that God is able to meet all my needs kept me going and able to keep my oath.

A male Dayton participant stated, "Being born and raised as a Christian had the first impact on my life. Doing the right thing has always been the way I run my life." A male participant in the Jos seminar referred to the Bible as his guide:

> The word of God has also been the beacon that is guiding me to keep the oath. Psalms 111, verse 11, says "Thy word have I had in my heart, that I might not sin against you." I pattern my life after the oath that I will abstain from corrupt practices. Joseph is a good example from the Bible. Daniel was also a man of integrity when he refused to obey the law of the king.

This participant concluded, "I was born a Muslim and later gave my life to Christ. That has an impact on my life before the seminar. I thank God for ANAC and what God is using ANAC to do worldwide."

A participant in the Abuja seminar related how she escaped being raped by her stepfather. She gave credit to her being well raised as a Christian by her father. She ran away from home and struggled to send herself to college. She kept her oath while in college and is satisfied with her life today, gainfully employed and happily married.

Influence of the ANAC Seminar

One of the objectives of ANAC is organizing workshops, conferences, seminars, symposia, and public lectures to sensitize and raise public awareness on bribery and corruption and the need to shun bribery, corruption, and all related vices in Nigeria. All the participants attended one of the seminars held in six different locations.

Commenting on the impact of the seminar, an Abuja male participant remarked, "The seminar opened our eyes through your examples. I was moved by the lectures and the examples given." Another Abuja male participant said: "The seminar has helped me to be firm in everything I do. Getting things the right way put my mind at peace. But before then, my conscience always bothers me."

Talking about conscience, another Abuja male participant disclosed, "the seminar played a key role in my life. It helped in my decision and strengthened the feelings I have against corruption. It gave me a conscience that pricks me if I am about to do something wrong."

A male participant in the Ibadan seminar specifically talked about the lectures:

> The lectures at the seminar were very exciting. I saw it as a potent and wonderful thing that will positively impact the nation, especially the youth. I knew I have to be part of the vanguard and do something about corruption.

A female participant in the Zaria seminar extended the benefits of the seminar to her children:

> At the time of the seminar, I was in the age of having children. Joining gave me a focus on how to guide my own children; I am happy they have all grown and make references to the way they were brought up, thanking me for talking about honesty and transparency in everything. That is the positive outcome of what the oath has done for me.

Another participant in the Ibadan seminar spoke about the seminar this way:

> On the day of the seminar that I took the oath, there was electric in the atmosphere. The caliber of the people that were there, the kind of statement and experiences that people shared about the need to get rid of corruption in Nigeria, make you feel that if you don't do it, nobody else will do it.

A male Jos participant told me that he was not aware of what the seminar would entail but when he realized that the seminar was actually to correct some anomalies in the country, he became interested. He said of the seminar, "I was exposed to the danger of corruption through the lectures and came to understand that if we wanted a better Nigeria in future, the process begins from us. I willingly took the oath." This participant concluded, "I remember vividly that in your bid to enlighten us of the danger of corruption, you wept. We were all moved." What a reminder of the day I wept for Nigeria!

Another male participant at the Jos seminar talked about the seminar and even commented on my speech:

> The seminar promoted integrity, truthfulness, holiness, and godliness. It has been helping me and also encouraging me to live my life above corruption. That day, I was determined to be truthful and made a fresh covenant with God against corruption. Your address and the examples about your life remind me of Psalm 78, verse 72. "So he fed them according to the integrity of his heart, and guided them by the skillfulness of his hands."

Another remarkable comment from a male participant at the Dayton seminar went this way:

> ANAC did a lot in the seminar I attended. When one takes an oath as required by ANAC I think it makes the individual come back. It is almost like being re-baptized. Anybody who takes such an oath and takes it seriously and takes it to heart will not join that type of a race in fostering corruption in any situation.

The participant concluded, "If all of us can get together and make commitment against corruption that commitment may have an impact on all of us and will trickle down into the fabrics of the society."

The Jos seminar brought back the memory of his late father to one participant:

> I attended ANAC seminar after my father died. Everything my father was telling me came back to my memory. I said to myself, "if my father has been telling me about this honest type of lifestyle that will help me, I must take this seminar seriously." Hence I took the oath.

Impacts of Taking the ANAC Oath

The impact of the oath on the participants is revealed in two dimensions from the interviews. There are those who reported that they kept their oath strictly and maintained it in the face of all temptations. Those are discussed below under the heading of "consistent impact." And there are those who, at one time or another, failed to honor their oath. Their experiences are discussed under "inconsistent impact."

Consistent Impact

A female participant in the Jos seminar who credited upbringing, religion, and the seminar for her strong determination against corruption talked about how her friends advised her to submit to her lecturers so she can easily pass. She rejected this negative impact and said: "After I attended ANAC seminar, I became stronger in my determination by refusing invitations from lecturers who invited me out." She explained that she and three other students came to the seminar from her university. "I talked about it in all my classes so that my lecturers and fellow students may know that I have taken an oath against corruption." The participant said that she could not get work after college. Friends have advised her on whom to see but she realized that seeing anyone would result in bribery or corruption. What did she do instead? "I am now back in school studying to become a nurse. This is a field that I know has a number of jobs available and I will get a job without compromising," she told me.

Another negative influence from peers was rejected by a female participant in the Abuja seminar. She talked about how she has been isolated by her colleagues in supervisory positions. "They exclude me from some projects because I will not compromise with the procedure or the corrupt outcome of the project either in term of award of contract or sharing undue profit after the contract." In regard to moving ahead in her job, she said that she has refused to bribe anyone for her promotion, which must have hampered her being promoted when due. When I asked what keeps her going, she answered: "My belief that God will always meet all my needs kept me going and make me able to keep my oath."

A male participant in the Jos seminar, a pastor who has had several temptations to break his oath, gave thanks to God for giving him the courage and wisdom not to fall for the temptation. His story is discussed below under episode.

A female participant in the Dayton seminar living in the United States disclosed that in her travels to and from Nigeria she had witnessed custom and immigration officers receiving bribes; she generally complied with this so that she could pass through without her luggage being inspected. She told me,

Since I have taken the oath, I have decided never to give bribe to anyone again. I believe corruption can be eradicated in Nigeria if more people take and keep the oath. If there is no giver, there will be no receiver.

A Dayton seminar male participant boldly told me "I have not violated any public trust. I have kept the oath and will continue to do so all my life. It has never been difficult for me to keep the oath. It is first nature for me." He told me of his political ambition in Nigeria. His goal is to provide a system that is accountable and honest to ensure stability. "I believe we can bring back the good old days where leadership is based on welfare of the society in providing adequate infrastructure and safety of life," he said. He credited his upbringing in a house where community, regional, and national leaders gathered to discuss what is good and not good for the nation. On the state of the nation, he said, "Unfortunately today's politicians use money to restructure the fundamental of values to suit their own ends. Money is taken away from funding schools and the standards fall while their own kids are studying abroad." He continued to lament the deplorable situation in Nigeria: "Jobs are not created. Hospitals are short of medications. Money from Nigeria is being used to buy properties in cities around the world." He ended with a recommendation:

> I believe we can find solutions to the problems of Nigeria. The solution has to go all the way back to the type of investment we are going to be making not only in families but also in education. When people are very well prepared, they become competitive. They have the capacity for individual initiative and can begin to regroup the economy. These types of individuals will end holding political offices, from the highest to the lowest, and bring idea that will benefit everybody.

Another male participant, who attended the Efon-Alaaye seminar while in university, got a job after graduating to manage a department. Not long after he began, his colleagues were advising him on how to make money illegally on the job to supplement his salary. He told me that, as he was contemplating joining them in their nefarious activities, he came across his ANAC membership card, and immediately the oath kicked in. The next time they came into his office to check on whether he was following their suggestions, he did not hesitate to tell them: "What you cannot get through a legal way, if you get it through illegal way, it will not benefit you." He warned them that if they were caught in any illegal practice they would face punishments. He informed me that there were two staff members he specifically advised against corruption. Two months later one of them was caught receiving a bribe and was dismissed. The other staffer, however, got closer to him and followed his advice to reject the path of bribery and corruption.

A male participant in the Ibadan seminar told me of how a strong commitment led him to confront bribe takers on many occasions. His story is also told below when I recount some specific episodes of oath-taker behavior. I asked if he has been tempted to give or receive a bribe since he took the oath. He commented:

> Since I took the oath, I have not had any temptation because for me, there is no temptation. I am already armed. Come rain or shine, I am not going to give you a bribe. So the issue of temptation does not come in.

Inconsistent Impact

This aftermath of oath taking is, regrettably, not unblemished. Two participants mentioned that circumstances pushed them not to be able to keep their commitment to the oath. A male participant in the Jos seminar worked for a private organization. As a manager in the company, he has to secure contracts for the company. In order to be able to secure contracts and maintain his job he had to give bribes on behalf of the company. He used a Hausa proverb to describe his action on behalf of the company, "If you are in a town where everybody has a tail, find a rope and tie it to look like a tail." He said he does not take kickbacks on his job because of his oath. But his action gave room to political, bureaucratic, and business corruption. When asked which of the three forms he was guilty of, he answered "all of the above."

The second participant who has had inconsistent success was also a male university student in the Jos seminar. He flouted his oath directly. He was able to keep the oath for 2 years while he was still in the university. He was privileged to teach in the university after graduating. He said to me that his university was one of the most corrupt in the nation.

> I was confronted by fellow lecturers to conform with the system in examination malpractices and favoring female students for an affair. I struggled very hard to keep my oath, lost some friends, thought of my moral upbringing, my religious background, but I failed to take the oath to the end.

He regretfully let this happen, as he soberly disclosed to me in our interview. This is a case of negative influence by peers. He stated, apologizing to me as he did, that he received bribes from male students and slept with female students, all to become part of the system because he felt he had to join the rest of his colleagues. Having been raised in a moral religious upbringing and having taken the ANAC oath, he told me that each time he violated his oath his conscience made him feel guilty. He claimed to have gone through a depression, which led him to resign from the teaching position after a year of falling into bad company.

Impact on Relation to Peers

Some of the participants spoke about peers' influence on their life after taking the oath. As narrated above, the participant who spent a year as a university lecturer was influenced to join the group of corrupt lecturers by his peers. There is no doubt in my mind that his university was full of many corrupt lecturers. I taught in a similar university in Nigeria for 8 years and can attest to the fact that it takes a disciplined mind not to be corrupted. This kind of disciplined mind was exhibited by that male participant in the Efon-Alaaye seminar whose new colleagues counseled him on the need to be corrupt in his new job. As mentioned, before he could make a decision to join or not to join, he happened to come across his ANAC membership card and the oath kicked in. Also two female participants in the Jos and Abuja seminars were able to ward off negative friends. They did not yield to the advice of their friends/colleagues to join into the corruption, and even parted ways with them. One told of how she could not find job after graduation and decided to study nursing since it is a lucrative field with plenty of opportunities and did not require bribery to enter.

Specific Episodes

Let us look more closely at some of the revealing experiences that I was told about in interviews. Some of the participants have been playing the role of resisters and concerned citizens since they took the oath. Empowered by the membership card, which they always carried, they have challenged government officials that are exploiting innocent people. These experiences are discussed under the heading of what I call "direct" and "indirect" episodes.

Direct Episodes

By "direct" I refer to when the participant reported experiences where she or he got fully involved in an episode of potential corruption. A male participant in the Jos seminar described a direct experience he encountered after taking the oath. As a pastor there were cases of some women coming to him for counseling in what he described as demeaning dresses. He used to accommodate such dressing before he took the ANAC oath, but he said that since he took the oath he has never hesitated in cancelling such appointments and telling them to come another day in a befitting dress. He informed me that many pastors have fallen into the temptation of having affairs with women in their congregation. He recalled two instances in the community where he lives. The participant also talked about his encounter with the police. He narrated how he was arrested by a policeman for driving through a traffic light that was not working. Upon demand of a bribe, he categorically told the policeman he does not give bribes because he has taken an ANAC oath against bribery. After explaining what ANAC is about to the policeman, he was reluctantly let go. On another occasion, he went to the police station to ask for the release of his friend who was arrested for a traffic offense. Upon demand of a bribe, he threatened to report the policeman to his superior, and his friend was released.

A male participant in the Ibadan seminar narrated that he was once traveling with his family and his daughter fell sick on the trip. He put her on the back seat of the station wagon in which they were traveling. He disclosed that a policeman at a checkpoint noticed the girl sleeping at the back seat and questioned him as to why she was sleeping there. The police demanded his driver's license and held on to it in anticipation of a bribe. This participant immediately pulled out his ANAC identification and told the policeman to return his driver's license or face being reported to his most senior officer through a phone call. "A senior police officer on the scene noticed what was going on, moved in and got my license from the policeman and returned it to me," he concluded.

A third direct episode involving the same Ibadan male participant was also with the police. His story in its entirety:

> One day, I was driving in a traffic hold up and a policeman walking towards me just opened my car and said let's go. After about a block he asked me to

park and requested for my driver's license. I gave him. He looked at it and said it has expired few days before. I looked at it and truly it has expired but I did not realize it. He told me to settle him for one third of what it will cost in fine if he should take me to the office. I asked why he stopped me of all the vehicles on the road. He said that the spirit directed him. I took out my ANAC card and accused him of asking me for a bribe. I told him the spirit directed him to a wrong person and he should therefore get out of my car. He wasted no time to get out after giving me my driver's license.

Another episode shows how some members of ANAC have carried the concept forward. A Zaria female participant started ANAC in the Catholic secondary school where she was teaching. She told me:

> The school where I taught was expensive and many of the children there came from rich families. I introduced ANAC and we made a blind boy the president. He once told me that the children were thinking of how their parents made the money to send them to such an expensive school, send them abroad on vacation during the holidays. It was a reality show for me.

She recalled how some parents were requesting information about ANAC though no student was asked to join because they were still under the joining age.

Another female participant in the Abuja seminar described her role after joining ANAC:

> I became the Northern Zonal Director. I was able to organize workshops in some secondary schools and National Youth Coppers camps. We received assistance and recognition from the government's anti-corruption commission. I thank God that some of these youth still believe in what I preached to them.

This participant arranged some of the seminars in which members of the National Youth Coppers joined ANAC.

Indirect Episodes

Some participants did not have a direct personal encounter with corrupt practice, but did observe others have that experience and did not just fold their arms in silence but instead took action. An Abuja female participant

4 RESEARCH FINDINGS: MOTIVES AND IMPACTS OF OATH TAKING   83

now residing in the United Kingdom narrated an experience she witnessed at the Nigerian Embassy in London.

> When I see something being done wrong, I get involved. Recently I was at the Nigerian Embassy in London to renew my passport. A lady came in and jumped the cue and was attended to. The lady in front of me noticed and protested blaming the officials. The officials in turn decided to delay the protester by attending to those of us behind her. After I got my passport renewed I approached the official and condemned their attitude to the lady and threatening that I will go and report to the ambassador about the incident. There and then they call the protester and attended to her need.

A male participant in the Dayton seminar recalled his experience at the international airport in Lagos during a visit to Nigeria. It was his first visit after he joining ANAC, and he made sure to have his ANAC identification card with him. Upon arrival at the immigration processing line for those with a Nigerian passport, he observed that the two lines available were very long and slow moving. He approached the window and inquired what was causing the delay. The officer told him they were short-staffed. As he was speaking with the officer, a superior officer approached him to find out what was going on. He asked the superior officer how they could be short-staffed when some uniformed custom officers were hanging around chatting when they should be in the designated positions attending to arrival passengers. He asked if the purpose of the delay was to create opportunity for some to bribe them and get out quickly. He then took out his ANAC membership card and told the superior officer he had taken an oath not to allow any corrupt practice to happen. He was hailed by the passengers as the officer directed three more of his staff to the counter, at which time the queues started to move along more.

A male participant in the Ibadan seminar has never left home without his ANAC membership card. Every oath-taking member is given an identification card showing their name and picture and the oath taken. Since bribery and corruption are clandestine activities, one assumes that police will not want to be in contact with anyone carrying anti-corruption identification. This has worked for me personally on many occasions. I have always passed through police checkpoints by showing my identification as an ANAC member. Whenever this participant showed the card at a police checkpoint, he said he had always passed through without problems. He narrated a story of how he ran into a checkpoint near a rail crossing. The traffic line was long, and he got out of his car to find out what was happening. To his surprise, two policemen were on the rail track where they stopped vehicles to check the vehicle and drivers documents. "I went to meet them and inquired why they were checking at the rail crossing. I immediately ordered them to move away from the track which they did without question." He then noticed the policemen held on to the driver's license and vehicle registration papers of a construction vehicle driver demanding the identification documents of the equipment being carried in the truck. As the driver was about to give them money to avoid the police delay, the oath-taker participant ordered the truck driver to stop and asked what was going on. The driver explained that since he did not have the required documentation for the equipment, the police had demanded money. The participant said he asked the police if it is the law that he should carry the documents for the equipment to which the policemen replied "no." He then introduced himself with his ANAC identification. "The police immediately handed the driver's documents to him and told him to go," he said. After that, the police removed the barricade they had put on the road and left as delayed vehicles now continued on their journey unimpeded.

Quantitative Summary of Motivating Factors for Oath Taking and Keeping

The above themes and sub-themes came from the transcripts of interviews in which the participants talked freely, guided by trigger points, which kept them focused on the objectives of the study. Table 4.1 outlines the framework for interview analysis using the responses to the trigger points. There are 11 trigger points or motivating factors represented by letters from A to K, and each category has three sub-triggers listed as 1, 2, and 3.

In Table 4.2 data from the 15 interviews are classified in terms of trigger points. Each trigger is defined by letters from A to K, while the participants are identified by numerals 1 through 15. The responses of each individual cut across the rows. In Table 4.3, the stories of all participants are quantified in terms of the factors deemed most significant.

4 RESEARCH FINDINGS: MOTIVES AND IMPACTS OF OATH TAKING

Table 4.1 Categories of motivating factors and participant responses (used for Tables 4.2 and 4.3)

A - Best reason for taking the oath
1. Awareness of corruption in Nigeria
2. Have always wanted to be part of a vanguard against corruption
3. Encouraged by the seminar

B - Events in the lives of participants before taking the oath
1. Never participate in corrupt practices
2. Have been a giver or receiver of corrupt practices
3. Have been both giver and receiver of corrupt practices

C - Events in the lives of participants after taking the oath
1. Never participate in corrupt practices
2. Have been a giver or receiver of corrupt practices
3. Have been both a giver and receiver of corrupt practices

D - Role of parents in the lives of participants
1. Parents very involved
2. Parents involved
3. Parents not involved

E - Impact of religion in the lives of participants
1. High impact
2. Moderate impact
3. No impact

F - Positive impact of peers
1. Very much
2. Moderately much
3. Not much

G - Negative impact of peers
1. Very much
2. Moderately much
3. Not much

H - Role of seminar
1. Played a great role
2. Moderate role
3. No role

I - Experiencing temptation
1. None
2. Occasionally
3. Very much

J - Able to keep the oath
1. All the time
2. Sometimes
3. Not able to

K - Talking to others about the oath
1. Always
2. Occasionally
3. Forgot about it

Table 4.2 Interview response data for motivating factors

Participant #	A	B	C	D	E	F	G	H	I	J	K	
1	1	1	1	3	1	1	3	1	3	1	1	m
2	2	1	1	1	1	1	3	1	3	1	1	f
3	2	1	1	1	1	1	3	1	3	1	1	m
4	1	1	1	1	1	1	3	1	3	1	1	f
5	1	1	1	1	1	1	3	1	3	1	1	m
6	2	1	1	1	1	1	3	1	2	1	3	f
7	3	2	1	1	3	3	3	1	1	1	1	f
8	2	1	2	1	1	1	3	1	2	1	1	f
9	1	1	1	1	3	1	3	1	2	1	1	m
10	3	3	2	2	2	1	1	1	3	2	1	m
11	2	1	1	2	1	1	3	1	3	1	1	f
12	2	2	1	1	1	1	3	1	2	1	1	m
13	2	1	1	1	1	1	3	2	3	1	1	m
14	1	1	1	1	1	1	3	1	2	1	1	m
15	2	1	1	1	2	1	3	1	3	1	1	m

Note: Identifications for factors A to K presented in Table 4.1

Table 4.3 Interview response frequency for motivating factors

Response #		A	B	C	D	E	F	G	H	I	J	K
	1	5 / 33%	12 / 80%	13 / 87%	13 / 87%	11 / 73%	14 / 93%	1 / (7%)	14 / 93%	1 / 7%	14 / 93%	14 / 93%
	2	8 / 53%	2 / 13%	2 / 13%	2 / 13%	2 / 13%	0 / 0%	0 / 0%	1 / 7%	6 / 40%	1 / 7%	0 / 0%
	3	2 / 13%	1 / 7%	0 / 0%	0 / 0%	2 / 13%	1 / 7%	14 / 93%	0 / 0%	8 / 53%	0 / 0%	1 / 7%

Note: Identifications for factors A to K are in Table 4.1

Summary of Findings on Motivating Factors

1. *Primary reason for taking the oath:* Though all the participants were aware of the degree of corruption in Nigeria, only five mentioned this as the primary reason for taking the oath. It may be

necessary for one to have a critical sense of ethics in the first place and disagree with corruption in order to take the oath. Others might know about corruption but they do not care or maybe did not define a problematic situation as corrupt. Eight participants had always wanted to be part of an anti-corruption vanguard, while two were encouraged to take the oath by participating in the seminar.

2. *Events in the life of the participants before taking the oath:* Twelve participants stated they had never participated in corrupt practices prior to the taking of the oath though they all had been victims of corrupt practices. Two indicated that they had given bribes before or had accepted a bribe before the oath. One participant had received and given bribes frequently prior to the taking of oath.

3. *Events in the life of the participants after taking the oath:* Thirteen have abstained from corruption since taking the oath, while one indulged in corruption for about a year as a university lecturer. Another gave a bribe to win contracts for his employer.

4. *Role of parents in the life of the participants:* Thirteen of the 15 participants highly commended the role their parents played in their life, while the other two barely commented on their parents' role, even when asked about this.

5. *Impact of religion:* Eleven participants credited their religion for the uprightness in their life. Two said that religion made some contributions, and two did not see religion as a significant influence.

6. *Positive impact of peers:* Fourteen participants disclosed that they are very selective about whom to befriend. They build positive friendships around themselves; hence, there is not much connection with wrongdoing associates. Two said friends moderately influence them, while one experienced a minimal positive influence of friends.

7. *Negative impact of peers:* Only one participant stated that the influence of peers made him got involved in corrupt practices after he had taken the oath. It took him a year and resignation from his job before he could free himself from the negative influence. The remaining 14 participants claimed that the negative influence of peers had no impact on them.

8. *Role of Seminar:* Fourteen participants applauded the significance of the seminars and called for more such sessions throughout the country. They all want to be part of ANAC seminars in the future. One participant said that the experience had moderately improved his determination to resist and work against corruption.
9. *Experiencing temptation:* One participant stated that temptation does not occur because he never gave it the chance to happen. He always had a strong determination against corrupt practices. Six disclosed occasional temptation, while eight stated temptation occurred regularly.
10. *Able to keep the oath:* Fourteen of the participants proudly claimed they have been able to keep the oath despite the temptation. One participant broke the oath over the course of 1 year as a university teacher.
11. *Talking to others about the oath:* Fourteen of the participants always talked to others, relatives, and friends about the oath and ANAC. One actually started a chapter of ANAC in the location where she was teaching. One had forgotten about ANAC until this interview, but nevertheless said that she has always kept her oath.

The narrative approach of storytelling via audiotape used in the study reveals the key aspects of the life experience of the participants with oath taking. The influence of upbringing, religion, the seminar, and peers stands out in the stories of the participants. The implications of these findings are discussed in the next chapter.

CHAPTER 5

Discussion of Findings: Taking, Keeping and Violating the Oath

Abstract The chapter begins with the interpretation of the findings in the previous chapter, emphasizing what the interviews revealed about motivations related to oath taking and oath keeping. These findings are discussed in relation to the following themes: participants' motives for deciding to take the oath; life experience of the participants in the struggle against corruption after taking the oath; commonalities and differences among the experience of the participants. The findings are related to the work of Thalhammer et al.'s framework of "Courageous Resistance," leading to conclusions about future research needs.

Keywords Factors producing behavior · Social context · Network · Preconditions · Giver/receiver · Arm folders · Iron fisters

In this chapter I reflect on the implications of my findings. The chapter is organized to discuss the following three themes:

1. What the findings reveal about motivations to take the oath;
2. Corruption experienced or witnessed after having taken the oath and consequent resistance; and
3. Commonality from the experience of the participants

What the Findings Reveal About Motivation

Why do people take a voluntary oath to shun corruption? The data of the study reveals that the four most frequently mentioned factors motivating the participants were:

- Upbringing (socializing);
- Religion (socializing);
- Awareness of corruption (critique of authority, but also critical social values);
- The seminar and becoming an ANAC member (networking).

Although these factors stand out as prominent, they are complexly related to other factors as well. In order to appreciate the meaning of these major factors I will use Thalhammer et al.'s (2007) theory of conditions that make it more likely for people to become resisters. I refer back to discussion in Chap. 2. Specific factors affecting the process of responding to injustice as found in the present study are shown in Fig. 5.1 They reflect and are related to the general categories of Thalhammer et al.'s theory.

While Thalhammer et al.'s (2007) theory refers to the preconditions consisting of internal factors of socializing, reinforcing, and modeling, this study's data reveals preconditions of upbringing (which is a form of socialization), religion, reinforcement, and modeling as motivating factors.

Upbringing

Twelve participants credited their parental upbringing as motivation for taking the oath. They narrated how their parents, in most instances, the father, had raised them toward a moral standard. They talked about how their parents were models for them. One participant disclosed that his father served many years in the Nigeria military but never enriched himself like many of others in his military ranks. Another participant remarked about how he observed his father being a peacemaker in the community as the house in which he grew up was a welcoming center for everyone. In other words these participants were ethically raised. As noted in Chap. 2, Velasquez (2002) defined ethics as "the discipline that examines one's moral standards or the moral standards of a society" (p. 15). Many of the participants explained how their parents guided them in doing what is right and refraining from dishonesty and corruption. The actions of the parents

5 DISCUSSION OF FINDINGS: TAKING, KEEPING AND VIOLATING THE OATH

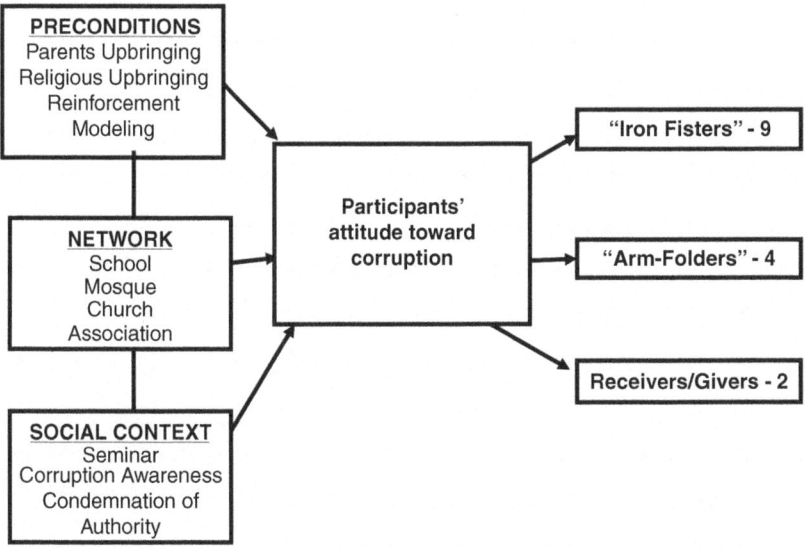

Fig. 5.1 Factors affecting and results of participants' keeping oath. (Adapted from K.E. Thalhammer et al. (2007 p. 17). Copyright 2007 by Palgrave Macmillan. Used with permission of Palgrave MacMillan)

are consistent with the theory of Thalhammer et al. (2007) where internal factors of socializing, reinforcing, and modeling come into play. Upbringing is part of Erikson and Kovalainen's (2008) traits of life experience and the support we receive as we grow and develop.

Religion

Eleven of the 15 participants claimed religion as a source of their morality in taking the oath and joining ANAC. Both Islam and Christianity were mentioned as the religion that boosted their morality. Two female participants mentioned that their father raised them strictly on religious codes. Though ANAC is a non-religious organization, religion plays a key role in its seminars. Religious clergy have been invited to all the seminars to speak on religious morality. Both Christian and Muslim Nigerians attended the seminars. Given that the large majority of Nigerians are religious, Awolalu (1976) suggests paying attention to religion as a possible inspiration for oath taking against corruption. The social value of religion is also noted by Adeniyi (2001) as an important factor in combating corruption. He suggested that religion dictates to its followers basic values intended to guide people toward living an idealistic lifestyle. This is consistent with Thalhammer et al. (2007) views on the importance of having a network comprising external factors of friends and organizations. The church and the mosque are gathering places for Christians and Muslims on Sundays and Fridays, respectively, worshipping, socializing, and networking and experiencing temperament traits and characteristics as noted by Eriksson and Kovalainen (2008).

Awareness of Corruption

The participants spoke about the effects of corruption in their country, and their stories indicate that they are concerned about lack of infrastructures such as adequate roads, water, and electricity, as well as about security, unemployment, sexual immorality, and lack of respect for humanity, among other dangers of corruption. Maslow's "Hierarchy of Needs" framework provides a window on this as those needs are distributed in his five-leveled pyramid. The concern in this study is not the hierarchy of unmet needs but the overall awareness and experience of injustice due to corruption in the lives of the participants and other Nigerians like them, which motivated them to action.

All 15 participants stated they were aware of the endemic state of corruption in Nigeria before they attended the seminar, but only 5 of them identified this awareness as the primary reason for taking the oath. Two participants indicated they made up their mind to join ANAC before coming to the seminar. Thalhammer et al. (2007) noted that several dimensions of the context of a situation can influence whether people become perpetrators or bystanders to injustice. Such dimensions—referred to as contextual factors—include living under difficult economic conditions, political violence, and trying life conditions. In relation to their rejection of the corrupt society all participants blamed the country's leadership and the government machinery for the exploding corruption in the country. In particular one participant in the Dayton seminar condemned the governments that have ruled Nigeria since the first military coup of 1966. A female participant in the Jos seminar referred to the police, immigration, and the custom officials as "robbers in uniform."

"The domestic climate is chaotic," a participant in the Abuja seminar noted. A female participant in the Zaria seminar, now raising her grandchildren in the

US, disclosed that she had used bribes to get her children educated and also to get a job when she was living in Nigeria.

Several authors have written about the corrupt climate in Nigeria. Smith (2006) wrote that the government-controlled oil industry in Nigeria is riddled with graft. Smith described the image of Nigeria as a basin of bribery, venality, and deceit. A World Bank study (Iarossi and Clarke 2011) concluded that 80 % of businesses in Nigeria had paid bribes to government officials—firmly supporting the opinion of the participants. Several authors—Dzoho (2007), Ejiofor (2010), and Hagher (2011)— have written about the magnitude of the corruption in Nigeria. Staub (1989) noted that living in such conditions is challenging and appears to increase people's feelings of injustice and powerlessness. One finds similarity in the context of Thalhammer et al.'s theory where external factors such as societal values, domestic and international climate advocacy networks, institutions, and rules form the bases of this context.

Critical socializing can lead to critical positioning toward authority, as in Thalhammer et al.'s (2007) model. Thalhammer et al. also made it clear that the attitude toward authority as well as ongoing activities within and outside the environment may lead to any of the three categories of behaviors—perpetrator, bystander, or a resister. "Individuals with this approach to authority actively formulate, evaluate, and question all policies in light of their values. They do not accept any authorities or laws as intrinsically legitimate" (Thalhammer et al. 2007, p. 33). The participants' narratives indicated they were willing to challenge authority. For example, this willingness was manifested in the attitude of a university female participant who refused to give in to negative pressures to give her body for a good grade. Even in an early life, a participant resisted by running away from her stepfather who had attempted to rape her, and she reported the attempted rape to other relatives—an act that took extraordinary strength. "The rape situation is very rife in Nigeria. There are adequate reports on daily bases of parents assaulting children, proprietors of schools assaulting pupils, grandfather raping grandchild" (Bimbolakemi et al. 2014, p. 472). Though the stepfather's action was also taboo, the female participant was unsure whether she would have the support of her family members when she rejected her stepfather as a parent because they easily could have blamed her for having seduced her stepfather. "In many social contexts, domestic violence, whether sexual, physical, or psychological, is supported by social norms such as cultural ideology which promotes the primacy of men over women in Nigeria" (Esere et al. 2009, p. 3).

The ANAC Seminar's Influence

The data also revealed the opinion of the participants about the seminars. All the participants described the seminars they attended as inspiring, encouraging, and motivating. Topics of lectures at the seminars were directed at the issues confronting Nigeria. Examples are: "Nigeria after the Nightmare," "The Leadership Nigeria Needs," "What Corruption Does to a Nation," "Mobilization for a Change at the Grassroots Level," "Spirituality Guidance in the Quran to an Honest Living," "Spirituality Guidance in the Bible to an Honest Living," "Complain Alone Shall not Suffice," and "No Giver, No Receiver." A participant noted that the topics were appropriate for the occasion and stated that he had not attended a lecture on these topics throughout his 4 years of study at the university. Participants also noted the caliber of people invited to give lectures at the seminar—this could be considered positive reinforcement. Thalhammer et al. (2007) allude to the fact that positive reinforcement by one or more people can strengthen an individual's values and understandings of what moral behaviors are and inspire action (p. 29). Speakers at the seminars were specifically selected to represent, among others, education, religion, authority, and royalty where possible. Each seminar included high-profile people, including Christian clergy and Muslim imams to administer the oath. Speakers at the inaugural launching at the Zaria seminar consisted of the president of the university at which it was held, the traditional ruler of the area, and the area commandant of the Nigerian Army who administered the oath with the Muslim and Christian clergies. Among the speakers at the Abuja seminar were the Honorable Minister who represents the President of the country, the chairman of the anti-corruption commission of the nation's Independent Corrupt Practices and Other Related Offences Commission (ICPC), and a Supreme Court justice who administered the oath. The guest speakers at the Dayton seminar included the Nigerian Ambassador to Canada, Nigerian Americans who were heads and directors of various organizations in the Dayton area, a Christian bishop, and a Muslim imam.

Invited speakers spoke about their life experiences and how they have been able to suppress the temptation to live a corrupt life. The presence of high-profile individuals at the seminars led the participants to feel as though they were not alone, especially considering that ANAC itself is a recognized organization that can provide a network. At the end of each seminar participants interacted with the guest speakers. Thalhammer et al. (2007) noted that such a network affects the likelihood that people will learn something important is happening and take it seriously (p. 28). They also considered networks to be social structures of ongoing relationships among individuals, groups, and institutions, which are interactive and result in an exchange of resources (pp. 27–28). ANAC has received tremendous support in term of materials, people, technology, and promotion from the Independent Corrupt Practices and Other Related Offences Commission (ICPC).

According to Thalhammer et al.'s (2007) theory, no single factor leads to the behavior of becoming a perpetrator, bystander, or resister. Rather, it is the combination of several factors. Upbringing, attitude toward authority, the desire to help others, and the domestic and international climate all contribute to the same force that, for example, led Paul Rusesabegina to save the lives of many Rwandans, as recounted in Thalhammer et al.'s stories of courageous resisters. Similarly, Sergeant Joseph Darby, who blew the whistle on the perpetrators of humiliation and torture of Iraq prisoners at Abu Ghraib, did not become a resister overnight. (Thalhammer et al., 2007, p. 53). So it has been for the resisters in this study that a combination of several factors led them to bravely confront corruption.

CORRUPTION EXPERIENCED OR WITNESSED AND CONSEQUENT RESISTANCE

Several events in the lives of the participants after taking the oath show the positive impact of the oath. Stories from the interview indicated how some participants confronted corruption upfront and did not yield to the demand of corruption either by the law enforcement agencies or authorities or entrapment by associates.

Nine out of the 13 participants who said they kept their oath can be categorized as resisters because they have stories to back this up. In his story, a male participant from the Ibadan seminar confronted authority on two occasions and stepped in to help others on one occasion. He did not yield to the police attempt to extort money from him when he was challenged for putting his daughter on the back seat of his car and when he was randomly stopped and police found that his driver's license had expired. He also stepped in at a police check point on a railway crossing to foil the police's attempt to solicit a bribe from a truck driver. He is a courageous resister who not only resisted on behalf of himself, but also to help others. This participant declared that he would challenge every unjust act he comes across.

A second participant—a pastor from the Jos seminar—refused to welcome women who did not dress properly into his office. On two occasions he deflated police attempts to solicit a bribe from him and from a friend. Being a pastor can be regarded as a social factor that demands exemplary behavior, given that the congregation will expect their leader to be a good example. "Social capital appears to be most significant when a person reaches a crossroad where he or she must decide to act against injustice or not" (Thalhammer et al. 2007, p. 29). He is also a resister.

As previously noted, a third participant from the Abuja seminar ran away from a stepfather who had attempted to rape her. After taking the ANAC oath she rejected her university's lecturers in their attempts to seduce her and made it known to her friends and those lecturers that she was under oath to abstain from corrupt practices. The attitude of this participant can be credited to positive reinforcement from the seminar. She had demonstrated resistance by escaping an immoral act from her stepfather, and the attendance at the seminar was an added value that strengthened her behavior and understanding of what moral behaviors are.

A fourth participant, also from the Abuja seminar, was prevented from participating in senior officials' deliberations of awarding contracts because she refused to be a part of inappropriate procedures in how the contracts were awarded. She experienced a delay in promotion; however, she also became a model for transparency in her office.

The fifth resister was an example of an incidental resister, one who steps in to help others in-group when authority displays acts of injustice. A male Dayton seminar participant noticed the immigration clearing line was moving slowly on arrival to Nigeria, and he asked an immigration officer about the reason for the situation. The participant was aware that this is the usual prelude to encourage bribery at the port of entry. The intervention led to the deployment of more immigration officers to the desks and faster clearance of travelers. The rest of the travelers were content to remain in line until it was their turn, while this participant decided not to be a bystander to a practice leading to an act of injustice. He most likely had witnessed such situations in the past before becoming a member of ANAC. Armed with his ANAC identification card he had the courage to go ahead and challenge the situation.

5 DISCUSSION OF FINDINGS: TAKING, KEEPING AND VIOLATING THE OATH   97

The sixth resister was an Abuja participant who resides in the UK. She was standing in the line to renew her passport at the Nigerian Embassy in London when a person skipped the line to receive immediate attention. An individual in the line protested, but was ignored by the attending official who then bypassed her when it was her turn. The Abuja seminar participant waited for her turn to get her passport renewed before expressing concern about the incident and threatened to report the case to the ambassador if the ignored protester was not given immediate attention. The action of the unknown resister must have encouraged her not to be a bystander. It should be noted here that this participant did not take action until she renewed her passport—thus she was a bystander for a period of time. At that point she was neither the direct perpetrator nor the victim. In Thalhammer et al. (2007) terms, she was a passive supporter of the perpetrator's action, though she may have disapproved the action or held no particular judgment. She was at a decisive crossroads where she was tasked with deciding whether to actively side with the victim or remain mute. After renewing her passport, she decided to challenge authority on behalf of the protester.

A female Jos seminar participant was the seventh resister. After taking the ANAC oath, she made sure this was well known by all her lecturers in the university, becoming vocal in all her classes about the oath against corruption. After graduating from the university she could not get a job because of her stance, yet would not yield to corruption. She therefore "enrolled in a nursing school to become a nurse since jobs are always available for nurses," she claimed. This is an example of an individual who shielded herself from possible perpetrators by making it known to everyone what she stood for. To further solidify her determination in preventing acts of injustice against her she decided to change professions instead of engaging in corrupt acts to secure a job.

A male participant in the Efon-Alaaye seminar was being oriented by co-workers in how to multiply his income through corruption. As he was about to yield to the pressure he found his ANAC membership card and decided to stay true to his oath instead. He became a resister, advising others to abstain from corruption.

The ninth resister, from the Dayton seminar, disclosed that formerly she was fond of bribing her way through the customs in Nigeria any time she went home on vacation because she often returned to the US with foods that were not allowed out of the country. However, after taking the ANAC oath, she stopped breaking the rules and no longer offered bribes to customs officials. An individual or group of people can be perpetrators. This participant has ceased giving bribes and now conformed to the law.

Commonalities from the Experience of the Participants

What do these resisters have in common? First they are all members of ANAC and carried the membership card, having taken the ANAC oath at the end of the seminar they each attended. Apart from not falling into the trap of corruption, these nine participants did not act as bystanders, except for the participant in London for a short period. Instead, they chose to take a moral position in a dangerous situation. Upon becoming aware of a grave injustice, nine resisters among the participants risked unknown dangers to prevent abuses of power. According to Thalhammer et al. (2007, p. 34), an individual who reacts to injustice, experiences six phases in the process of acting as a courageous resister.

1. Notice that something is happening;
2. Interpret what they have seen as just or unjust;
3. Decide whether they should take personal responsibility;
4. Consider various responses and decide on a course of action,
5. Take their decided course of action;
6. Maintain their chosen course of action, reassessing whether to continue.

Even when the participant stories were not explicitly presented in terms of these evolutionary six junctions where people must make decisions, it seems plausible that the resistance was the result of a clear choice of strategizing about how to live up to their values. Though we do not know for sure if they became resisters only after taking the oath, it seems clear that the oath or membership in ANAC helped them to resist.

We can look at the activities and inactivities of the 15 participants in light of what Kelman and Hamilton (1989, p. 113) described as role, rule, and value orientations:

- Roles orientation— people who feel it is their place in society to obey and support authority by conforming and that the requirement to follow authority overrides other moral principles.

- Rules orientation—people who fear troubles or the cost of not conforming to laws and see rules as paramount.
- Value orientation—people who are most likely to challenge injustice.

The nine resisters are value-oriented people who were aware of what was happening and interpreted it as injustice. The resister who saw traffic held up at a railway crossing recognized this as wrongful and took action after deciding to take personal responsibility. The action of the resister who foiled the attempt of the Nigerian immigration officer to create an opportunity for injustice acted in a similar manner. They both recognized corrupt behavior and decided on a course of action. The resister at the Nigerian Embassy in London was in a similar situation as the first two resisters but decided to delay her action to suit her purpose. The university ladies who made it known to their friends and lecturers that they were under oath also went through the six junctions Thalhammer et al. (2007) described. They all took the risks of becoming resisters because they were not afraid of the danger that might follow their actions. These are cases of making a choice at the crossroads.

The oath or membership in ANAC was ignored by two participants who did not keep their oath, thus becoming what Thalhammer et al. call perpetrators. One participant works for a private company, and it is his responsibility to secure contracts for the company. In order to secure contracts, he bribed government officials and made deals on behalf of his company. The participant's actions fall into Ksenia's (2008) three types of corruption:

- Bureaucratic corruption when officials take bribes before performing services;
- Political corruption when elected politicians use their position of power to influence decisions after taking bribes;
- Grand-scale corruption where heads of state, ministers and top officials take bribes and misuse their power for a gain.

When asked which of the three categories of corruption he subscribed to on behalf of his company, he answered "all of the above" because everyone from top officials to politicians and office clerks benefited from the bribes his company dished out. He claimed he had to do it to keep his job and keep the company functioning. Although the participant was not directly benefitting by committing the crime, he was doing it on behalf of his company, a decision he made at a crossroad.

The second participant's corrupt practices were self-inflicted actions. As a result of brilliant academic performance at his university, he was appointed as an assistant lecturer. Though he had taken the ANAC oath while a student, he succumbed to a new work environment rife with temptations and illicit practices and became corrupted after he took the teaching position. He told me that his university is the most corrupt in the nation, and there was peer pressure on him to be like most of the lecturers. He became a victim of "friends" and coworkers in his network consistent with the adapted theory of Thalhammer et al. (2007). A network in and of itself does not help unless it is a network of like-minded in action *against* corruption. According to the participant, in that university's culture, lecturers take bribes from students and have affairs with female students. He confessed being involved in these activities for 2 years. This is an indication that taking the oath alone does not guarantee that one refrains from corruption. "Positive reinforcement by even one other person can strengthen an individual's values and understandings of what moral behaviors are and inspire action" (Thalhammer et al., p. 29).

The two perpetrators, like the nine resisters, noticed that something wrong was happening and interpreted this as unjust. At their crossroads, peer socializing, the influence of in-group friends, and the climate in which they worked, led them to choose the path of perpetrators.

Four other participants did not indicate whether they witnessed or experienced any act of injustice. Though they may not be perpetrators, they are also not resisters. Thalhammer et al. (2007) described individuals like this as:

> People who simply choose not to act though they do feel responsible for helping address the problem. They may know what harm is being done, disapprove of it, and feel responsible for acting, but they interpret the situation as so overwhelming or risky or hopeless that they dare not resist it. (p. 4)

Two of the remaining four participants live in Dayton; two were in Nigeria where one expects they should be confronting corrupt activities regularly since everyone talked about the prominence of corruption everywhere, all the time. Could the reason for their not speaking up in the face of corruption be an effect of *my* methodology? Did I focus so much on the purpose of the study, finding what motivated participants to take the oath against corruption, that I neglected other questions that could open more windows? If the participants had talked more of their experiences or that of their relatives, before and after the oath, there could have been "hurt" as motivation. This could be addressed in a future study.

VALUES OF REVELATION IN TERMS OF ANTI-CORRUPTION STRUGGLE

These cases indicate that people can abstain from corruption if they make up their mind to do so. It is significant that they can feel the power of a collectivity by being someone who would not leave home without the ANAC membership card. Carrying the card and using it when relevant is one possible way of responding to injustice. According to Thalhammer et al. (2007), this type of "resource can help counter obstacles to courageous resistance and change calculations as to what is or is not possible" (p. 28). Staub (1989) referred to these people as prosocial value oriented. These are people having a positive disposition toward human beings and who are concerned about their welfare in the face of injustice.

At the same time there was the case of a participant who felt he was a victim of negative peer pressures and defaulted in his oath. However, when he experienced the conscientious guiltiness of breaking the oath, he got back on track. This illustrates the relevance of taking the oath. Would he have continued to be anti-corrupt without the organization? Are those who did not take the oath likely to be involved in corrupt practices? This is a dilemma for ANAC and other anti-corruption organizations. It will be necessary to find out during ANAC seminars why those who did not take the oath made that decision. One can also consider the high number of 13 out of 15 participants who have abstained from corruption since taking the oath. Were they telling me the truth? I must work on the assumption that since they took the oath not to lie, they are also going to tell me the truth.

HOW MY FINDINGS RELATE TO MOTIVATION THEORY AND THALHAMMER ET AL.'S THEORY OF RESISTANCE

This study is about standing up against corruption, first being motivated to take an oath against corruption and then becoming a resister to acts of injustice. According to Dawson cited in Thompson and McHugh (2002), there is something internal that motivates behavior. Organizations have applied content or process theories to modify the behavior of their employees. Similarly Thalhammer et al. (2007) include these as "Factors affecting the process of responding to injustice" (p. 17).

I discussed Maslow's hierarchy of needs theory as perhaps accounting for the motivational factors applicable to the participants who stepped forward to take an oath against corruption. Data from the study reveals the concern of the participants about the lack of infrastructure, security, and jobs, because of the high degree of immorality that exist in Nigeria. These are all part of lower and upper needs in Maslow's theory as diagrammed earlier in Fig. 2.1. These needs are part of what Thalhammer et al. consider to be a process of perceiving and responding to injustice that may create or not create perpetrators, bystanders, and courageous resisters in term of injustice actions. The participants in this study are adults who in the course of their lives have socialized with family, at school, mosque, or church, which could have some bearing on their lives. Living in a society where corruption is the order of the day the attitudes of the participants toward authority could be positive or negative depending on the examples they have been exposed to during their formative years.

Thalhammer et al. noted that choices individual make when they become aware of the occurrence of wrongs depend on who they are, who they know, and the nature of their environment. The upbringing, the religion, and parental reinforcing are internal motivation that might have encouraged the nine resisters among the participants.

Research Questions for the Future

The purpose of this study was to find out why people take a voluntary public oath to shun corruption in all its ramifications. The answer to this question creates sub-questions, which this study also tried to answer. What happened in their life to make them come to that decision? How does taking the oath impact their lives? What role do family, religion, and peers play in the way they give meaning to the oath? In the study for this book I have only scratched the surface of answering these questions. Each sub-question could be a research question for future studies.

My study took place at a time when a radical Jihad organization in Nigeria was terrorizing the country. Opposing Western education, the Boko Haram terrorist organization has maimed and killed thousands of people, both Christians and Muslims. They have committed atrocities in Northern Nigerian cities and have murderously bombed even in the nation's capital of Abuja and in an ever-growing array of other communities across the nation. As a result the study was done through telephone interview. Could there have been differences in the results if I had been able to spend longer time on the phone and probe more into the life history of the participants? Nine of the participants lived in Nigeria at the time of the interview. I spent more time with the remaining six living outside Nigeria. Could a face-to-face interview have provided more intimate information than I now have? Future studies should consider the methodology and the environment in the nation. The results of the study that upbringing, religion, awareness of corruption, and ANAC's seminar served as motivating factors to taking an oath against corruption raise further questions to examine.

The topic of religion should be explored further by finding out the kind of socialization that takes place in churches and mosques after prayers and what events as a result have led to the morality and the rejection of authority. Future research should also explore how the situational context of Nigeria—particularly the difficult life conditions—has affected the individuals on the level of feelings of injustice and powerlessness. It will be beneficial to find out at what age and level participants begin to formulate, evaluate, and challenge authorities about acts of injustice in order to determine whether they had been resisters before joining ANAC.

Finally, the findings of the study should be useful in future seminars to be conducted in Nigeria and other countries where Nigerians are living. It will also help in developing guidelines for several anti-corruption programs in Nigeria and other African countries.

CHAPTER 6

Policy and Practical Implications for Future Anti-Corruption Programs

Abstract The concluding chapter addresses the policy and practical implications of the study for future anti-corruption public and civil programs in Nigeria and other African countries where corruption is systemic. The role of civil organizations in combating corruption is summarized with specific emphasis on the role of the Association of Nigerians against Corruption. The future plan of ANAC is outlined as the chapter closes with thoughts that bind the entire study.

Keywords Future implications · Civil organizations · Brain drain · Economic growth · Ehusani pledge · Ken Saro-Wiwa · Margaret Mead

In this chapter I discuss the policy and practical implications of the study for future anti-corruption public and civil programs in Nigeria and other African countries where corruption is systemic.

Despite all the laws and regulations against corruption in Nigeria, the only way to reduce corruption is to address it at all phases. The findings of my study show that individuals can become resisters to injustice through upbringing, religion, and positive peers. According to Adelugba (2013), in present-day Nigeria, the state of socioeconomic development dictates the necessity to harness all resources for the betterment of the people. Everyday corruption in Nigeria as exposed in the stories of the participants, indicates that survival in Nigeria is a huge challenge compared to advanced countries of Western Europe and North America. The ubiquity of wrong-doing has led many professionals from Nigeria to emigrate, thus causing brain drain. If more people are exposed to ANAC's approach to combating corruption at the grassroots level, there is hope for reduction in corruption and reversal of the brain drain that has made Nigerians of many fields to flee their homeland.

Brain drain involves the loss of skilled intellectual and technical labor and of talent through the movement of such labor to more favorable geographic, economic, or professional environments. It leads to the depletion of intellectual and technical personnel and, gradually, of energy or resources to sustain and improve the economy and all institutions that create a prosperous and good society. It can be seen in the deteriorating situation of the institutions of higher learning as discussed by one of the Dayton participants. It is visible in major industries. The private sector is denied the experience that emigrated people would have brought to bear on the economy. Mba and Ekeopara (2012) relate a depressing assessment indicating how the downward spiral into increasing corruption relates to the loss of highly trained and moral professionals:

Nigeria cannot achieve long-term economic growth by exporting its natural resources. The professionals that are emigrating out of Nigeria include those with technical expertise, entrepreneurial and managerial skills, and in the new world order, economic growth is driven by people with knowledge. It is the most talented citizens that should lead the people create wealth and eradicate poverty. Hence their absence increases the endemic corruption and makes it easier for the looters to continue in the act.

As a result of the flight from corruption, this brain drain makes the negative economic conditions that led to corruption increasingly bad.

Some of the participants in this study expressed concern for the deplorable economy in the country. Such is the cause of lack of employment, increase in crime, lack of safety, and other deficiencies in meeting the needs described and categorized in Maslow's theory.

The root cause of brain drain in Nigeria according to Adelugba (2013) lies in the successive leaderships and governments that have demonstrated, very convincingly, that the interests of Nigeria and its citizens were never their priority. They relentlessly pursued their own agenda. This is reflected in Thalhammer et al.'s (2007) theory of internal preconditioning resulting in the attitude toward authority.

According to the Nigeria Health Workforce Profile (Labiran et al. 2008), a total of 3552 doctors emigrated out of Nigeria in 2007.

Adelugba (2013) noted that pre- and post-independence Nigeria had a monumental increase in educational opportunities for Nigerians both within and outside the country and consequently increased rate of workforce development. I was a beneficiary of the post-independence opportunities. The expectation was that all these would translate into recognizable improvement in infrastructural development and the betterment of life for all Nigerians. To some extent, this was beginning to happen before venal politics and military interventions redirected the course of Nigeria development and history as discussed in Chap. 1. The government, through its ineptitude and lack of vision, has turned its populations with productive capacities into willing sophisticated slaves in foreign lands.

After studying abroad for 12 years, I returned to Nigeria to serve the government for 10 years. But as the state of the nation became deplorable with corruption and indiscipline becoming the order of the day, I went back to the US for another 27 years. Now, I am taking the struggle against corruption at the grassroots level back to Nigeria. The research for this book has enhanced my belief that appealing to the mindset of individuals as was done with the participants in the study will be one successful way to reduce corruption in Nigeria.

To boost the economic growth of Nigeria, the brain drain needs to be reversed. In the words of one of the participants: "I believe we can bring back the good old days where leadership is based on welfare of the society in providing adequate infrastructure and safety of life;" Mba and Ekeopara (2012), echoed this in their writing:

> To reverse brain drain and boost economic growth, the Nigerian government should create a conducive environment for investment that will ensure employment opportunities and reduce poverty. It should also put in place good institutional framework, maintain zero tolerance for corruption. (p. 5)

Every participant lamented the lack of infrastructure in the country. Mba and Ekeopara (2012) further recommended the provision of the much-needed infrastructures such as good health care systems, affordable and functional education, water supply, electricity, security, stable energy, and telecommunication facilities. These are the essential ingredients that make life worth living.

Role of Civil Organizations in Combating Corruption

There is no one solution to the problem of corruption in Nigeria. The government has its role to play as explained above alongside the civil society. Each anti-corruption organization should have a focus. The Association of Nigerians against Corruption (ANAC) focuses its attention on getting individuals to reject corruption, hence the idea of starting from everyone as grassroots level.

Every participant in my study expressed their desire to be part of future seminars. This desire promotes an opportunity for networking. A strong network of friends and organizations is an additional important factor that affects the process of responding to injustice as theorized by Thalhammer et al. (2007) and confirmed in this study. Thalhammer et al. stated further that networks affect individual response in three ways:

1. Provision of necessary knowledge and model alternative interpretations;
2. Creating social capital to support and reaffirm courageous resistance;
3. Making crucial resources available.

ANAC was founded in 1984 as a non-government organization to campaign against corruption from the grassroots level. Our campaign continues to map Nigeria into six operational zones.

Each zone is represented by a director reporting to the headquarters located at the Leadership Institute in Jos, in the central Plateau State. Political or religious disturbances might prevent smooth operations occasionally. The urge to shun corruption begins at the individual level as is demonstrated by the narratives of some of the participants in this study. This operation will make coordination of networking possible. Members of the association will be able to liaise with the office nearest to them. ANAC will extend its campaign strategies to both secondary and elementary schools for youths of ages 6–15. Most of the participants explained that they have been motivated from youth to live an honest life by their parents. Workshops and seminars to be run in high and elementary schools will include parents. Also religion plays a key role in the life stories of the participants. Although not taking responsibility for teaching religion as such, ANAC will be conducting workshops and seminars in churches and mosques. In doing so ANAC, acknowledges the strong and continuing role of religion in the Nigerian peoples' lives and will be able to connect to the way religion is experienced and can support anti-corruption.

ANAC will establish an "Academy for Character and Leadership Development" that will run 2- to 3-week seminars for Nigerian youths of secondary and university levels. ANAC shall also engage in grassroot outreach campaigns by going into the market places, motor parks, and other public places where people who could not have the opportunity to attend the seminars could be reached. If corruption is essentially everywhere, so too must be an organization combating it!

There are about 50 non-government anti-corruption organizations in Nigeria under the umbrella of the Zero Corruption Coalition. Organizations should be encouraged to network with each other, which, according to Thalhammer et al.'s (2007) theory, improves conditions that encourage resistance.

Over the years, scholars, activists, and international organizations have identified elements that when present can assist in winning the war against corruption in Nigeria. My study has taken this down to the most basic level of the individual, showing the powerful influence of oath taking, while also revealing that much more will be needed for the approach to succeed. Corruption cannot be fought only by civil organizations; one needs a larger initiative as well, including:

1. Political will and commitment to fight corruption;
2. A legislative framework for transparent and accountable government;
3. A comprehensive strategy that is systematic, consistent, focused, publicized, non-selective, and non-partisan by both the government and civil organizations;
4. Protection of whistle blowers and resisters;
5. Mobilization for social re-orientation at all levels of the educational system and in faith-based organizations;
6. Freedom of the press;
7. Adequate remuneration and necessary equipment for workers to reflect the responsibilities of their position and living wage;
8. A code of ethics bounding all government and private employees at all levels;
9. Well-publicized bounty rewards for acts of honesty.

Ehusani (2003) in an essay on *Religion and Corruption in Nigeria* wrote that Nigerians need a "wholesale doctoring of our individual and collective consciences" (para. 28) to make them more sensitive to the concept of right and wrong and of good and evil. He proposed an approach somehow similar to the ANAC's approach of oath taking. He suggested that Nigerians recite the following lines daily until corruption is wiped out of Nigeria:

> I pledge my commitment to the emergence of a new Nigeria, recognizing that greed and avarice are a cancer that eats its own host to death; that corruption ultimately kills not only the victims, but also the perpetrators, and that unless we change our course we are bound to end up where we are headed.
>
> I pledge my commitment to the emergence of a new Nigeria, recognizing that righteousness exalts a nation, but that sin is a reproach to a people; and that where there is no vision the people soon perish.
>
> So help me God to renounce these evils in myself, and to fight them in Nigeria with all the resources you have bestowed upon me. (Ehusani 2003, para. 30–33)

The goal of getting individuals to abstain from corruption in all its ramifications is based on the principle that it takes a giver and a receiver, a perpetrator and at times the victims, to commit the injustice of corruption. One of the ways that Nigerians can realize their dream and hope is enshrined in Chapter II of the Constitution of the Federal Republic of Nigeria (1999).

> The State shall...(a) harness the resources of the nation and promote national prosperity and an efficient, a dynamic and self-reliant economy; (b) control the national economy in such manner as to secure the maximum welfare, freedom and happiness of every citizen on the basis of social justice and equality of status and opportunity. [Constitution of Federal Republic of Nigeria 1999, Part. II, § 16 (1)]

This will encourage Nigerians in all walks of life to make public declarations against bribery and corruption and keep the oath. This has been the task of the Association of Nigerians against Corruption. The association shall continue to promote and support other groups and organizations engaged in activities similar to the one being pursued by ANAC and others in Africa and the world. ANAC shall conduct research and procure, publish, and disseminate information on the negative impact of bribery and corruption on Nigerian nation and its people.

Final Thoughts

> Some have already cast themselves in the role of villains, some are tragic victims, some still have a chance to redeem themselves. The choice is for each individual.
> – Saro-Wiwa, K. (1995). *Statement before execution*

My study brought out the stories of 15 individuals who have chosen to redeem themselves and the settings they live and work in. These stories hardly begin to tell about the many other experiences of about 1000 ANAC oath takers overall. Those are also just a tiny fraction compared to the 2.6 million in public service in Nigeria today (El-Rufai 2015) and many thousands more who have essential public responsibilities. Meanwhile, as I finish this book, millions of everyday people have voted in another presidential election, despite the personal dangers and decades of disappointment with rampant political corruption during and after Nigeria's elections. The very fact that a terrorist sect like Boko Haram has formed and acts so violently may have been enabled, in part, by widespread corruption, a point made in Chayes (2015) *Thieves of State*.

Yet the people continue to go to the polls and hope, despite experience and evidence, for change. Among them is the miniscule number of ANAC oath takers, a seemingly insignificant speck in Nigeria's turbulent history. The stories of the 15 men and women who were the participants in my study seem so small in comparison to the huge fact of universal corruption. But their choices are already making history, reminding us of the famous words often attributed to anthropologist Margaret Mead: "Never doubt that a small group of thoughtful, committed citizens can change the world; indeed, it's the only thing that ever has" (as cited in Textor 2005, p. 12).

References

American Heritage College Dictionary. (1993). Boston: Houghton Mifflin.
Mister Johnson (novel). In *Wikipedia, The Free Encyclopedia.* Retrieved from http://en.wikipedia.org/w/index.php?title=Mister_Johnson_(novel)&oldid=548443821
Achebe, C. (1959). *Things fall apart.* New York: Anchor Books.
Adelugba, J. (2013). *Brain drain: The Nigerian situation.* Retrieved from www.gamji.com/article
Adeniyi, N. O. (2001). War against corruption in Nigeria: The need for Islamic approach. *Journal of Arts & Social Sciences, 2*(1), 15–25.
Adewale, S. A. (1987). *Crime: African traditional religion.* Ibadan: Abe Books.
Adler, L. (1977). *Maslow's hierarchy of hiring pyramid according to Adler.* Retrieved from Ere.net/2012/06/28.
Ajayi, F.A. (1962). *Milestone in Nigerian history.* Ibadan: University Press.
Alderfer, C. (1969). An empirical test of a new theory of human needs. *Organizational Behavior and Human Performance, 4*(2), 142–175.
Apitzsch, U., & Siouti, I. (2007). *Biographical analysis as an interdisciplinary research perspective in the field of migration studies.* University of York. Retrieved from http://www.york.ac.uk/res/researchintegration/Integrative_Research_Methods/Apitzsch%20Biographical%20Analysis%20April%202007.pdf
Atkinson, R. (1998). *The life story interview.* London: Sage.
Awolalu, J. O. (1976). What is African traditional religion?. *Studies in Comparative Religion, 10*(2), 1–10.
Ayegboyin, D., & Ishola, S.A. (1997). *African indigenous churches: An historical perspective.* Retrieved from http://irr.org/african-indigenous-churches-historical-perspective

Azikiwe, N. (1994). *My odyssey: An autobiography*. Lagos: Spectrum.
Banuri, S., & Eckel, C. C. (2012). Experiments in culture and corruption: A review. World Bank Policy Research Working Paper 6064. Retrieved from https://openknowledge.worldbank.com/bitstream/handle/10986/9355/WPS6064.txt?sequence=2
Barnes, L.B. (1960). *Organizational systems and engineering groups*. Boston: Harvard Graduate School of Business.
Bauer, T. N., & Erdogan, B. (2009). Perceived over qualification and its outcomes: The moderating role of empowerment. *Journal of Applied Psychology*, 94, 557–565. doi:10.1037/a0013528.
Bell, D. (2002). *Ethical ambition*. New York: Bloomsbury.
Bimbolakemi, O., Falana, B. A., & Olotu, O. (2014). Prevalence of violent sexual assault on South West Nigeria girls. *European Scientific Journal*, 10(7), 471–481. Retrieved from http://eujournal.org/index.php/esj/article/download/2997/2823
Blackburn, K., Bose, N., & Haque, M. E. (2010). Endogenous corruption in economic development. *Journal of Economic Studies*, 37(1). doi:4-21. doi:10.1108/01443581011012234.
Bloor, M., & Wood, F. (2006). *Biographical methods*. London: Sage.
Boakye-Sarpong, K. (1989). *Witchcraft: Myth or reality*. Lusaka: Multimedia.
Bourdieu, P. (1986). The biographical illusion. *Actes de la Recherche en Science Sociales*, 62(3), 69–72.
Buchner, S., Freytag, A., Gonzalez, L., & Guth, W. (2008). Bribery and public procurement: An experimental study. *Public Choice*, 137, 103–117. doi:10.1007/s11127-008-9315-9.
Carr, E. C. J., & Worth, A. (2001). The use of the telephone interview for research. *Nursing Times Research*, 6(1), 511–524.
Charmaz, K. (2006). *Constructing grounded theory*. Thousand Oaks: Sage.
Chayes, S. (2015). *Thieves of state: Why corruption threatens global security*. New York: W.W. Norton.
Coker, M. A., Ugwu, D. U., & Adams, J. A. (2012). Corruption and direct investment in Nigeria. *Global Advanced Research Journal of History, Political Science, and International Relations*, 1(4), 79–88.
Connolly, P., Keller, D. R., Leever, M. G., & Cox-White, B. (2009). *Ethics in action: A case-based approach*. Chichester: Wiley-Blackwell.
Constitution of the Federal Republic of Nigeria. (1999). Retrieved from http://www.wipo.int/wipolex/en/text.jsp?file_id=179202
Adeyemi, S. (2013). Create special anti-graft agency for corrupt politicians *Punch*. Retrieved from http://www.punchng.com/news/create-special-anti-graft-agency-for-corrupt-politicians-senator/
Creswell, J. (1998). *Qualitative inquiry and research design: Choosing among five traditions*. Thousand Oaks: Sage.

Cullen, R. (2008). *The poverty of corrupt nations.* Toronto: Blue Butterfly.
Dike, K.O. (1999). *Trade and politics in the Niger Delta, 1830–1835.* Oxford: Oxford University Press.
Dreher, A., Kotsogiannis, C., & McCorriston. (2007). Corruption around the world: Evidence from a structural model. *Journal of Comparative Economics,* 35(3), 443–466. doi:10.1016/j.jce.2007.07.001.
Dzoho, P. (2007). *Nigeria salvation plan: The aftermath of militocracy, and the stepping-stones to historical greatness.* Abuja: Bilex.
Ehusani, G. (2003). Religion and corruption in Nigeria. Retrieved from www.georgeehusani.org/home/index.php/papers-and-essays/232-religion-andcorruption-in-Nigeria
Ejiofor, T. (2010). *Nigeria in quagmire.* Abuja: Xibris Corporation.
Ejizu, C. I. (1986). *Ofo, Igbo ritual symbol.* Enugu: Fourth Dimension.
Ejizu, C. I. (n.d.) *African religions and the promotion of community living in Africa.* Retrieved from http://afrikaworld.net/afrel/index.html
El-Rufai, N. A. (2015, January 18). Reforming our dysfunctional public service. Retrieved from http://www.el-rufai.org/reforming-our-dysfunctional-public-service/
Eriksson, P., & Kovalainen, A. (2008). *Qualitative methods in business research.* London: Sage.
Esere, M. O., Idowu, A. I., Durosaro, I. A., & Omotosho, J. A. (2009). Causes and consequences of intimate partner rape and violence: Experience of victims in Lagos, Nigeria. *Journal of AIDS and HIV Research,* 1(1), 1–7. Retrieved from http://unilorin.edu.ng/publications/iadurosaro/Esere%20et%20al.pdf
Fabiyi, O., & Adetayo, O. (2012, November 5). My removal was to destroy EFCC– Ribadu. *Punch.* Retrieved from http://www.punchng.com/news/my-removal-was-to-destroy-efcc-ribadu/
Fagbadebo, O. (2007). Corruption, governance and political instability in Nigeria. *African Journal of Political Science and International Relations,* 1(2), 028–037.
Falola, T. (1999). *The history of Nigeria.* Westport: Greenwood.
Fisher, J. (1998). *Nongovernments: NGOs and the political development of the Third World.* West Hartford: Kumarian Press.
Fitzgibbin, W. (2015, February 10). Files open new window on $182-million Halliburton bribery scandal in Nigeria. *International Consortium of Investigative Journalists.* Retrieved from http://www.icij.org/project/swiss-leaks/files-open-new-window-182-million-halliburton-bribery-scandal-nigeria
Frank, A. W. (2010). *Letting stories breathe: A socio-narratology.* Chicago: University of Chicago Press.
Fredrick Herzberg motivational theory. (n.d.). Retrieved from http://www.businessballs.com/herzberg.htm

Gardner, W. L., Avolio, B. J., Luthans, F., May, D.R., & Walumba, F. (2005). "Can you see the real me?" A self-based model of authentic leader and follower development. *Leadership Quarterly*, 16(3), 343–372. doi:10.1016/j.leaqua.2005.03.003.

Garlington, D. B. (1995). Oath taking in the community of the new age. *Trinity Journal*, 16(2), 139–170.

Gastil, R.D. (1986). *Freedom in the world: Political rights and civil liberties, 1985–86*. Westport: Greenwood.

George, B., Sims, P., McLean, A. N., & Mayer, D. (2007). Discovering your authentic leadership. *Harvard Business Review*, 85(2), 129–138.

Ghana Anti-Corruption. (n.d.). Retrieved from www.ghanaanti-corruption.org

Gopinath, C. (2008). Private corruption: Recognition and justification. *Journal of Business Ethics*, 82, 747–754. doi:10.1007/s10551-007-9589-8.

Guba, E. G., & Lincoln, Y. S. (2005). Paradigmatic controversies, contradictions, and emerging confluences. In N. K. Denzin & Y. S. Lincoln (Eds.). *The Sage handbook of qualitative research* (3rd ed., pp. 191–215). Thousand Oaks: Sage.

Gyimah-Brempong, K. (2002). Corruption, economic growth, and income inequality in Africa. *Economics of Governance*, 3(3), 183–209. doi:10.1007/s101010200045.

Habib, M., & Zurawicki, L. (2001). Corruption and foreign direct investment. *Journal of International Business Studies*, 33(2), 291–307. doi:10.1057/palgrave.jibs.8491017.

Hagher, I. (2011). *Nigeria after the nightmare*. Lanham: University Press of America.

Haidt, J. (2012). *The righteous mind*. New York: Pantheon.

Hall, D. T., & Nougaim, K. E. (1968). An examination of Maslow's need hierarchy in an organizational setting. *Organizational Behavior and Human Performance*, 3(1), 12–35. doi:10.1016/0030-5073(68)90024-X.

Hanlon, J., Pettifor, N., & Travis, A. (2000). *Kicking the habit. Finding a lasting solution to addictive lending and borrowing and its corruption side effects*. London: Jubilee Coalition.

Harrison, R. (1966). *A conceptual framework for laboratory training*. Washington, DC: National Training Laboratory.

Heylighen, F. (1992). A cognitive-systemic reconstruction of Maslow's theory of self-actualization. *Systems Behavioral Research Science*, 37(1), 39–58. doi:10.1002/bs.3830370105.

Hiller, H. H., & DiLuzio, L. (2004). The interviewee and the research interview: Analysing a neglected dimension in research. *Canadian Review of Sociology*, 41(1), 1–26. doi:10.1111/j.1755-618X.2004.tb02167.x.

Iarossi, G., & Clarke, G.R.G. (2011). *Nigeria 2011: An assessment of the investment climate in 26 states*. Washington, DC: World Bank. Retrieved from http://documents.worldbank.org/curated/en/2011/06/16613534/nigeria-2011-assessment-investment-climate-26-states

Idowu, E. B. (1973). *African traditional religion*. Maryknoll: Orbis.
Inglehart, R., Basanez, M., & Moreno, A. (1998). *Human values and beliefs: A cross-cultural sourcebook: Political, religious, sexual, and economic norms in 43 societies: Findings from the 1990–1993 World Values Survey*. Ann Arbor: University of Michigan Press.
Ishichei, E. (1976). *A history of Igbo people*. London: Palgrave MacMillan.
Kalu, H. (2011). *Together as one: Interfaith relationships between African traditional religion, Islam and Christianity in Nigeria*. Bloomington: iUniverse.
Karnieli-Miller, O., Strier, R., & Pessach, L. (2009). Power relations in qualitative research. *Qualitative health research, 19*(2), 279–289.
Kelman, H., & Hamilton, V.. (1989). *Crime of obedience: Toward a social psychology of authority and responsibility*. New Haven: Yale University Press.
Kenny, C. (2006). Narrative inquiry. In B. L. Wheeler (Ed.), *Music therapy research* (pp. 416–428). University Park: Barcelona.
Knox, S., & Burkard, A. (2009). Qualitative research interviews. *Psychotherapy Research, 19*(4–5), 566–575. doi:10.1080/10503300802702105.
Kofele-Kale, N. (2006). Change or the illusion of change: The war against official corruption in Africa. *George Washington International Law Review, 38*(4), 693–747.
Ksenia, G. (2008). Can corruption and economic crime be controlled in developing countries and if so, is it cost-effective?. *Journal of Financial Crime, 15*(2), 223–233. doi:10.1108/13590810866917.
Kvale, S. (1996). *Interviews: An introduction to qualitative research interviewing*. Thousand Oaks: Sage.
Kvale, S., & Brinkmann, S. (2009). *InterViews: Learning the craft of qualitative research interviewing*. Thousand Oaks: Sage.
Labiran A., Mafe, M., Onajole B., & Lambo E. (2008). *Health workforce country profile for Nigeria*. Abuja: Africa Health Workforce Observatory.
Laing, A. (2012, October 2). Malawi's Joyce Banda takes 30 per cent cut salary. *Johannesburg Daily*, p.1.
Lambsdorff, J. G. (1998). An empirical investigation of bribery in international trade. *European Journal of Development Research, 10*(1), 40–59. doi:10.1080/09578819808426701.
Lambsdorff, J. G. corruption affects persistent capital flows. *Economics of Governance, 4*(3), 229–243. doi:10.1007/s10101-002-0060-0.
Landy, F., & Becker, J. (1987). Motivation theory reconsidered. *Research in Organizational Behavior, 9*, 1–38.
Lederman, D., Loayza, N. V., & Soares, R. R. (2005). Accountability and corruption: Political institutions matter. *Economics and Politics, 17*(1), 1–35. doi:10.1596/1813-9450-2708.
Lewis, E. (1835). *A dissertation on oaths*. Philadelphia: Hunt.

Josselson, R. Lieblich, A. (Eds.). (1995). *The narrative studies of lives*. London: Sage.
Lieblich, A., Tuval-Mashiach, R., & Zilber, T. (1998). *Narrative research: Reading, analysis and interpretation*. Thousand Oaks: Sage.
Lincoln, Y. S., & Guba, E. (1985). *Naturalistic enquiry*. Beverly Hills: Sage.
Louw, D. (1998). *Ubuntu. An African assessment of the religious order*. Paper presented at Twentieth World Congress of Philosophy. Boston. Retrieved from http://www.bu.edu/wcp/Papers/Afri/AfriLouw.htm
Madu, N.E. (2013, December 2). Gender, politics and corruption: The Nigerian case. *News24*. Retrieved from http://m.news24.com/nigeria/MyNews24/Genderpolitics-and-corruptionThe-Nigerian-case-20131202
Magessa, L. (1997). *African religion: The moral traditions of abundant life*. Maryknoll: Orbis.
Mamdani, M. (1996). *Citizen and subject: Contemporary Africa and legacy of late colonialism*. Princeton: Princeton University Press.
Maslow, A. (1943). A theory of human motivation. *Psychological Review*, *50*(4), 370–396. doi:org/10.1037/h0054346.
Mauro, P. (1995). Corruption and growth. *Quarterly Journal of Economics*, *110*(3), 681–712. doi:10.2307/2946696.
Mayer, D. M., Nurmohamed, S., Treviño, L. K., Shapiro, D. L., & Schminke, M. (2013). Encouraging employees to report unethical conduct internally: It takes a village. *Organizational Behavior and Human Decision Processes*, *121*(1), 89–103. doi:10.1016/j.obhdp.2013.01.002.
Mba, P., & Ekeopara, C. (2012). "Brain drain:" Implication for economic growth in Nigeria. *American Journal of Social Issues and Humanities*, *2*(2), 41–47.
Mbiti, J. (1990). *African religions and philosophy* (2nd ed.). Oxford: Heinemann.
McMillan, J., & Wergin, J. (2010). *Understanding and evaluating educational research*. Upper Saddle River: Pearson.
Merrill, B., & West, L. (2009). *Using biographical methods in social research*. Thousand Oaks: Sage.
Miles, M., & Huberman A. (1994). *Qualitative data analysis: A source book of new methods*. Thousand Oaks: Sage.
Miller, R., & Brewer, J. (2003). *The A–Z of social research*. Thousand Oaks: Sage.
Mo, P. H. (2001). Corruption and economic growth. *Journal of Comparative Economics*, *29*(1), 66–79. doi:10.1006/jcec.2000.1703.
Musselwhite, K., Cuff, L., McGregor, L., & King., K. M. (2006). The telephone interview is an effective method of data collection in clinical nursing research: A discussion paper. *International Journal of Nursing Studies*, *44*(6), 1064–1070. doi:10.1016/j.ijnurstu.2006.05.014.
Nielsen, K., & Moreland, J. P. (1990). *Ethics without God*. Buffalo: Prometheus.
Korieh, C. J. Njoku, R. C. (Eds.). (2007). *Missions, states, and European expansion in Africa*. New York: Routledge.

Oduyoye, M. (1997). The African experience of God through the eyes of an Akan woman. *The Way, 37*(3), 195–206. Retrieved from http://www.aril.org/african.htm

Ojukwu, C. C., & Shopeju, J. O. (2010). Elite corruption and the culture of primitive accumulation in 21st-century Nigeria. *International Journal of Peace and Development Studies, 1*(2), 15–24.

Oluyitan, F. (2007). *Africa yesterday and today*. Bloomington: Author House.

Oluyitan, F. (Host) & Azikiwe, N. (Guest). (2013, August 13). Interview with NnamdiAzikiwe, [Television broadcast]. In *International Insight*. Dayton: DATV.

Onuoha, F. C. (2010). The Islamist challenge: Nigeria's Boko Haram crisis explained. *African Security Review, 19*(2), 54–67.

Otite, O. (1986). On the sociological study of corruption. F. Odekunle (Ed.), *Nigeria: Corruption in development* (pp. 11–19). Ibadan: Ibadan University Press.

Otusanya, O. J. (2011). Corruption as an obstacle to development in developing countries: A review of literature. *Journal of Money Laundering Control, 14*(4), 387–422.

Polkinghorne, D. E. (1994). Reaction to special section on qualitative research in counseling process and outcome. *Journal of Counseling Psychology, 41*(4), 510–512. doi:10.1037//0022-0167.41.4.510.

Rainey, H. (2001). *Work motivation*. R.T. Golembiewski (Ed.), *Handbook of organizational behavior* (pp. 19–39). New York: Marcel Dekker.

Ramphele. M. (2012). *Conversations with my sons and daughters*. Johannesburg: Penguin.

Rauch, J., & Evans, P. B. (2000). Bureaucratic structure and bureaucratic performance in less developed countries. *Journal of Public Economics, 75*(1), 49–71. doi:10.1016/S0047-2727(99)00044-4.

Ricks, S.D. (1999). Oaths and oath-taking in the Old Testament. In D.W. Parry & S.R. Ricks (Eds.), *The temple in time and eternity* (pp. 49–50). Provo: FARMS. Retrieved from http://publications.maxwellinstitute.byu.edu/fullscreen/?pub=1086&index=3

Rijckeghem, C. V. B. (2001). Bureaucratic corruption and the rate of temptation: Do wages in the civil service affect corruption, and by how much?. *Journal of Development Economics, 65*(2), 307–331. doi:10.1016/S0304-3878(01)00139-0.

Roberts, B. (2011). *Biographical research*. New York: Open University Press.

Sampson, I. T., & Decker, H. L. (2010). Gender and corruption: Understanding the increasing role of Nigerian women in corrupt practices. *Gender and Behaviour, 8*(2), 3117–3142. doi:10.4314/gab.v8i2.61937.

Saro-Wiwa, K.B. (1995, November 10). *Statement before execution*. Retrieved from http://www.colorado.edu/journals/standards/V5N2/ESSAYS/wiwa.html

Schatzman, L., & Strauss, A. L. (1973). *Field research: Strategies for a natural sociology.* Saddleback: Prentice-Hall.

Schwandt, T. A. (2001). *Dictionary of qualitative inquiry* (2nd ed.)). Thousand Oaks: Sage.

Sherlock, S. (2002). Combating corruption in Indonesia? The ombudsman and the assets auditing commission. *Bulletin of Indonesian Economic Studies, 38*(3), 367–383. doi:10.1080/00074910215532.

Shermer, M. (2004). *The science of good and evil: Why people cheat, gossip, care, share, and follow the golden rule.* New York: Henry Holt.

Shleifer, A., & Vishny, R. (1993). Corruption. *Quarterly Journal of Economics, 108*(3), 599–617. doi:10.2307/2118402.

Shuy, R. W. (2003). In-person versus telephone interviewing. J. A. Holstein & J. F. Gubrium (Eds.), *Inside interviewing: New lenses, new concerns* (pp. 175–193). Thousand Oaks: Sage.

Singer, P. (2000). *Writings on an ethical life.* New York: Ecco.

Smith, D. J. (2006). *A culture of corruption: Everyday deception and popular discontenting Nigeria.* Princeton: Princeton University Press.

Sohl, S. (2004). *Kohlberg's theory and his critics.* [PowerPoint slides].Retrieved from http://www.slideserve.com/saul/kohlberg-s-theory-and-his-critics

Sparkes, A. C. (1994). Life history and the issue of voice: Reflections on an emerging relationship. *International Journal of Qualitative Studies in Education, 7*(2), 165–183. doi:10.1080/0951839940070205.

Staub, E. (1989). *Roots of evil: The origin of genocide and other group violence.* Cambridge: Cambridge University Press.

Steers, R., & Porter, L.W. (1987). *Motivation and work behavior.* Columbus: McGraw-Hill.

Strauss, A., & Corbin, J. (1990). *Basics of qualitative research: Grounded theory procedures and techniques.* London: Sage.

Swamy, A., Knack, S., Lee, Y., & Azfar, O. (2001). Gender and corruption. *Journal of Development Economics, 64*(1), 25–55. doi:10.1016/S0304-3878(00)00123-1.

Tedli, E. (1995). *Sankofa: African thought and education.* New York: Peter Lang.

Textor, R.B. (2005). Introduction. M. Mead (Ed.), *The world ahead: An anthropologist anticipates the future* (pp. 1–31). New York: Berghahn.

Thalhammer, K., McFarland, S., Glazer, P., O'Loughlin, P., Glazer, M., Shepela, S.,& Stottzfus, N. (2007). *Courageous resistance: The power of ordinary people.* New York: Palgrave Macmillan.

Thiroux, J. P., & Krasemann, K.W. (1977). *Ethics: Theory and practice.* Encino: Glencoe.

Thompson, P., & McHugh, D. (2002). *Work organisations: A critical approach.* Houndmills: Macmillan.

Transparency International. (2004). *Global corruption report 2004*. London: Pluto Press.
Transparency International. (2006). *Global corruption report 2006*. London: Pluto Press.
Transparency International. (2014). *Corruptions perceptions index 2014*. Berlin: Transparency International. Retrieved from http://files.transparency.org/con tent/download/1856/12434/file/2014_CPIBrochure_EN.pdf
U.S. Department of State, Bureau of Democracy, Human Rights & Labor, (2012). *Country reports on human rights practices for 2012: Nigeria*. Retrieved from http://www.state.gov/j/drl/rls/hrrpt/2012humanrightsre port/index.htm?dlid=204153&year=2012#wrapper
Udo, B. (2012, May, 27). At Democracy Day church service, Jonathan, ministers decline to say "amen" to prayer against corruption. *Premium Times*. Retrieved from http://www.premiumtimesng.com/news/5314-at_democracy_day_ church_service_jonathan_ministers_refuse_to_com.html
UNESCO. (2010). *Nigeria, UNESCO on poverty in Nigeria. The 2010 Global Monitoring Report*. Retrieved from http://allafrica.com/stories/printable/ 201001280540.html
United Nations Office of Drugs and Crime. (n.d.). *UNODC's action against corruption and economic crime*. Retrieved from http://www.unodc.org/ unodc/en/corruption/index.html?ref=menuside
Van Vuuren, H. (2002). Corruption, perception and foreign direct investment: Counting the costs of graft. *African Security Review*, *11*(3), 67–75. doi:10.1080/10246029.2002.9627970.
Velasquez, M., Andre, C., Shanks, T., Meyer, S., & Meyer, M. (2010). *A framework for ethical decision making*. Retrieved from http://www.scu.edu/ethics/ practicing/decision/framework.html
Velasquez, M. G. (2002). *Business ethics: Concepts and cases*. Upper Saddle River: Prentice Hall.
Wood, G., Wood, J., Zeffane, R. Fromholtz, M., & Fitzgerald, J. (2006). *Organisational behavior: Core concepts and applications*. Milton: Wiley.
Ying, S. (2004). Regime and curbing corruption. *China Review*, *4*(2), 99–128.
Zhao, J. H., Kim, S. H., & Du, J. (2003). The impact of corruption and transparency on foreign direct investment: An empirical analysis. *Management International Review*, *43*(1), 41–62.

INDEX

A
Abacha, Sanni, 12
Abdullahi, Ango, 57
Able to keep the oath, 79, 88
Abubakar, Abdulsalam, 12
Abubakar Tafawa Balewa University, 58
Abu Ghraib, 95
Abuja
   female participant, 70–74, 77, 80, 82, 92, 96–97
   killings in, 62
   launch of ANAC, 58
   male participant, 74–75
   oath-takers, 58, 69
Academy for Character and Leadership Development, 109
Adeyemi, Smart, 17
Advanced Fee Fraud and Other Fraud Related Offences Act, 17
African Church Denomination, 9
Agabi, Kanu, 58
Aguyi, Ironsi, 12
Ahmadu Bello University, 4, 57
Akanbi, Justice Mustapha, 16
Akintola, Ladoke, 12
Akogun, Lt. Col. Tunde, 57
Alu, Katsina, 58

ANAC membership card, 78, 80, 83, 97, 101
ANAC Seminars, 57–59, 88, 101
Annan, Kofi, 30
Anti-corruption commissions, 31
Anti-corruption crusades, 16
Anti-corruption decrees
   in Hong Kong, 31
   in Indonesia, 31
   in Singapore, 31
Anti-corruption oath, 58, 69
Anti-corruption policies, 32
Anti-corruption struggle, 101
Asset recovery, 29
Association of Nigerians against Corruption (ANAC), 3–5, 17, 32, 50, 57, 108
Awareness of corruption, 90, 92, 103
Awolowo, Obafemi, (AG), 10, 12, 15
Azikiwe, Nnamdi, 10–11

B
Babangida, Ibrahim, 12
Balewa, Tafawa, 11–12
Banda, Joyce, 25
Banks and other Financial Institutions Act, 17

Barro, Robert, 27
Bello, Ahmadu, (NPC), 10, 12
Bible, 35, 41, 44, 74, 94
Biographical illusion, 55
Biographical methods, 55
Biographical research, 55, 68
Birth of political parties in Nigeria, 10
Blundo, Giorgio, 25
Boko Haram, 34, 37, 61–62, 102, 111
Brain drain, 71, 106–107
Bribery, 26, 77
  ANAC oath, 81
  campaign against, 5
  clandestine activity, 83
  community culture, 36
  country's image, 15
  image of Nigeria, 93
  negative impact of, 110
  oath against, 36
  public awareness on, 5, 74
  public declarations, 5, 110
  regulation on, 22
  state affairs, 2
Brown, Ron, 22
Buhari, Muhammadu, 4, 12–13, 57
Business International Indices of Corruption (BI), 27
Bystanders, 37–38, 92–93, 95–98, 102

C

Christianity, 8, 43, 91
CIA Report to the US Congress, 22
Civic organizations, 3, 32, 107–110
Civil war, 12
Coal, 14
Coalition government, 11
Coercion, 9
Coker, J. K., 9
Colonial inheritance, 47
Colonialism, 7–9
Columbine, 14
Conceptualization of human needs, 35
Consistent impact, 76–79
Constitution of Nigeria, 11
Constructionism, 55
Corruption
  awareness of, 70–71, 90, 92, 103
  bureaucratic, 22, 26, 28, 99
  business, 26
  categories, 26
  cause of, 22
  civil services and, 23–24
  counter and prevent, 28–32
  danger of, 75
  definition, 2–3
  degree of, 86
  determination against, 77
  development and, 20–25
  effects of, 27
  emergence of, 13–16
  FDI, effects on, 28
  fight against, 31
  financial, 17
  forms of, 25
  gender and, 24
  genesis, 7–9
  grand, 22, 99
  impact of, 27–28
  initiatives against, 16–18
  Laws on (31/99), 31
  magnitude of, 93
  manifestations of, 25–28
  negative economic growth, 21
  origin of, 50
  penalties, 15, 17
  political, 22, 26, 99
  prominence, 100
  red tape and, 27
  resistance, 95–98
  role of civil organizations, 107–10
  socio-political, 13

symptoms, 22
types of, 22, 99
universal occurrence, 1
upsurge of, 50
voluntary oath against, 32
wage war, 3, 16
women and, 24
women presence, 24
zero tolerance for, 107
Corruption Perception Index (CPI), 21, 27
Corruption Practice Investigation Bureau (CPIB), 31
Corrupt Practices and Other Related Offences Act, 16
Country Risk Review (CRR), 20
Courageous Resistance, 36
Courageous resisters
  injustice actions, 102
  likelihood of, 37
  motivating factor, 37
  stories of, 95
Crude oil, 14
Culture of Corruption, A, 15

D
Data analysis, 66–68
  coding, 67
  systematic coding, 67
Data sampling, 59–60
  criterion, 60
  opportunistic, 60
  snowball, 60
Dayton, Ohio, 5, 32, 58–59, 71–74, 76–78, 83, 92, 94, 96–97, 100, 106
De Sardan, Jean-Pierre Oliver, 25
Diamond, 14
Dishonesty, 2, 70
Domestic violence, 93
Drug trafficking, 31

E
Economic and Financial Crimes Commission (EFCC), 16–17
Economic growth, 21, 27, 106–107
Efon-Alaaye
  female participant, 73
  male participant, 71, 78, 80, 97
  oath-takers, 58
  participants, 59
  seminar, 58
Ego satisfaction, 35
Ehusani pledge, 109
Episodes, 68, 70, 79–84
  direct, 80–82
  indirect, 82–84
Ethical behavior, 39–40
  motivations for, 43
Ethics, 18, 20, 32, 35–36
  code of, 109
  definition, 38, 90
  development of, 40–41
  as motivating factor, 38–40
  notion of, 41
  oath taking, 42
  religion and, 43
  religious, 72
  study of right and wrong, 40
  universal aspect of, 41
  violation of, 42
Ethics Without God, 43
Experiencing temptation, 88

F
Failed Banks Recovery of Debts and Financial Malpractices in Banks Act, 17
Financial Action Task Force, 22
Financial scandals, 15
Foreign Direct Investment (FDI), 28
Fraudulent medicines, 31

126　INDEX

G
GALLUP International, 20
Galvao, Gil, 22
Gandhi, 36
Ghana Anti-Corruption
  Coalition, 31
Global Competitiveness Survey
  (GCS), 20
Global Monitoring Report
  (GMR), 13
Goal-setting theory, 32
Gold, 14
Government stability, 23
Gowon, Yakubu, 12

H
Habibie, 31
Halliburton case, 23
Hebrew Scriptures, 43
Hohn Milton, 43
Human trafficking, 31

I
Ibadan
  male participants, 59, 72, 75, 79,
    81, 83, 95
  oath-takers, 58
Idris, Alhaji Shehu, 57
Immorality, 2, 50–51,
  92, 102
Impact in relation to peers, 80
Impact of oath taking, 68
Impact of religion, 66, 87
Impact of taking ANAC
  oath, 96–98
Imperialism, 8
Inconsistent impact, 77, 79–80
Independent Commission against
  Corruption (ICAC), 31
Independent Corrupt Practice
  Commission (ICPC), 16, 58,
    94–95
Indianapolis Police Department, 7
Indirect rule
  outcome of, 9
  policy of, 8
Influence of ANAC seminar, 74
Institutional efficiency, 27
International airport, Lagos, 83
International Country Risk Guide
  (ICRG), 20, 23–24
International Labor Organization
  (ILO), 24
Interview
  biographical-narrative, 57
  face-to-face, 60–62, 68, 103
  life story, 4
  in-person, 60–61
  recorded, 65
  situation, 61
  structured, 55
  telephonic, 59–62, 68, 103
  transcribed, 64
  transcription of, 65
  unstructured, 55
Islam, 8, 10, 91

J
Jesus Christ, 36
Johannesburg Telegraph, 25
Johnson, Sirleaf-Ellen, 25
Jonathan, Goodluck, 13
Jos
  female participant, 77, 80, 92, 97
  killings in, 62
  male participant, 72–77, 79, 81
  oath-takers, 58
  pastor from, 96
Journalism, 7, 10

K
Kano, Aminu, (NEPU), 10
Kerry, John, 15

L
Lagos Weekly Record, 10
Leadership Institute, 58, 108
Lee, Jong-Wha, 27
Likert Scale, 24
Lincoln University, 10
Living to ethics and moral standards through oath, 42
Local Authorities, 13
Locke, John, 41
Lugar, Richard, 7
Lugard, Frederick, 8
Lugard, Lord, 8

M
Macaulay, Herbert, (NCNC), 10
Maiduguri, 62
Mandela, 36
Maslow's Theory of Motivation, 33–36
Mass Mobilization for Social Justice and Economic Recovery (MAMSER), 16
Mbiti, John, 45–47, 49
Mead, Margaret, 111
Member check, 65
Migrant smuggling, 31
Militant Islamic sect, 62
Military control, 23
Military coups, 12, 16
Military interventions, 12, 107
Milton, John, 43
Miscellaneous Offences Act, 17
Misuse of power, 2
Mohammed, 36
Money laundering, 16, 22, 25, 31
Money Laundering Act, 17
Money Laundering Prohibition Act, 17
Moral behaviors, 100
Moral depravity, 2
Moral standards, 38–39, 67
  categories of, 41
  components of, 39
  development of, 40–41
  ethics, 38
  features of, 39
  oath taking, 42
  understanding of, 39
  violation of, 39
Motivating factor, 37–40, 44, 68, 70–76, 71
  corruption awarenes, 70–71
  religion, 73–74
  ubpringing, 72–73
Motivation, 32–38
Muhammad, Muritala, 12
My story, 54

N
National Association of Nigerians and the Cameroons (NCNC), 10
Nationalism, 9–11
National Open Apprenticeship (NOA), 16
National Orientation Agency, 16
Negative impact of peers, 87
Network, 18, 20, 28, 31, 92–94, 100, 108–9
Network of Journalist Against Corruption, 31
Nigeria's first military coup, 92
Nigeria in Quagmire, 11
Nigerian Broadcasting Corporation, 6
Nigerian Embassy, London, 83, 97, 99

Nigerian League of Bribes
    Corner, 3
Nigerian Morning Post, The, 6
Nigerian National Council
    (NNC), 10
Nigerian Youth Service
    Corps, 58
No giver no receiver, 78, 94
Northern Elements Progressive
    Union (NEPU), 10
Nuhu, 17

O

Oath taking, 20, 29, 32, 44
    aftermath of, 79
    ANAC's approach, 110
    Christian values in, 50
    critics, 44
    discouraged in Bible, 44
    ethics, 42
    God-centered approach, 35
    impact of, 76–80
    influence of, 50, 109
    investigations against
        corruption, 33
    key concept, 6
    member's ID card, 83
    motivating factors, 84–88
    participants life events, 87–88
    peers' influence, 80
    primary reason, 86
    religion and, 43–51, 92
    religion as a inspiration, 43
    sworn affirmation, 43
Obasanjo, Olusegun, 3, 12, 16,
    30, 58
Okotiebo, Festus, 12
Old Testament, 43
On Christian Doctrine, 43
Organized crime, 31

Orientations, 98
Oyo State Ministry of Education,
    Ibadan, 58

P

Paradigm of study, 56
Parents in the life of participants, 87
Participants after oath, 87, 95
Participants before oath, 69, 87
Participants in the study, 33, 36, 38,
    40, 54, 107
Perpetrators, 37, 59, 92–93,
    97–100, 102, 110
    decision of, 36
    meaning of, 37
    passive supporters, 38
    whistle on, 95
Perversion, 2
Physiological-economic
    needs, 35
Physiological needs, 33
Piaget, Jean, 41
Piracy, 31
Population, 5, 9, 58–59
Positive impact of peers, 87
Preconditions, 37, 90
Preventive policies, 29
Primary reason for taking oath, 86

Q

Quantitative research standards, 59

R

Rape, 93
Rationalism, 41
Reinforcement theory, 32
Religion in African culture, 45
Religious belief, 73

Religious clergy, 91
Religious Morality, 40
Religious practice, 45
Research findings, 41
Resistance to White Rule, 9
Resisters, 37–38, 93, 100
   definition, 37
   protection of, 109
   role of, 80
   theory of conditions, 90
   value-oriented, 99
Robbers in uniform, 92
Robertson, Sir James, 11
Rusesabegina, Paul, 95

S
Saro-Wiwa, Ken, 111
Sectionalism, 13
Self-actualization, 33–35, 47
Shagari, Shehu, 12
Social contexts, 55, 93
Socio-economic development, 105
Sokoto caliphate, 8
Sources of data, 4
Standard & Poor, 20
Stories Breathe, 4
Story-telling, 4, 88

T
Talking to others about the oath, 88
Tarka, Joseph, (UMBC), 10
Terrorism, 31
Tesler, Jeffrey, 23
Theory of Resistance, 101–102
Things Fall Apart, 47
Tin, 14
Transitional advocacy networks, 37
Transparency International, 2–3, 21, 26–28

Transparent women leaders, 25
Tribalism, 13

U
Ubuntu, 49–50
United Middle Belt Congress (UMBC), 10
United Nations Convention against Corruption, 29
United Nations Office of Drugs and Crime (UNODC), 2, 31
University of Abuja, 58
University of Ibadan, 58
University of Jos, 58
Upbringing, 6–7, 20, 50, 54, 56, 67–68, 72–73, 77–80, 88, 90, 102–103, 105

V
voluntary obligatory oath, 44

W
Wahid, Abdurrahman, 31
War Against Indiscipline (WAI), 4, 16
West African Frontier Force, 8
West African Pilot, 10
Wildlife and forest crime, 31
World Bank, 14, 21, 24, 93
World Development Report (WDR), 20
World Values Survey, 24

Y
Yar'Adua, Umaru, 13

Z

Zaria, 4, 57–58, 62–63
 female participant, 75, 82, 92
 participants, 59
 speakers, 94
 traditional ruler of, 57
Zero Corruption Coalition (ZCC), 18, 109
Zero tolerance, 107

The manufacturer's authorised representative in the EU is Springer Nature Customer Service Centre GmbH, Europaplatz 3, 69115 Heidelberg, Germany. If you have any concerns regarding our products, please contact ProductSafety@springernature.com

Printed and bound by CPI Group (UK) Ltd, Croydon, CR0 4YY

23/03/2026

02076380-0001